PROMOTION OF LEARNING IN INDIA

PROMOTION OF LEARNING IN INDIA:

BY EARLY EUROPEAN SETTLERS, UP TO ABOUT 1800 A.D.

NARENDRA NATH LAW,
WALTER K. FIRMINGER

GYAN

Published by

Gyan Publishing House
5, Ansari Road
Daryaganj, New Delhi-110002
Phone: 011-47034999, 9811692060
E-mail: books@gyanbooks.com

Distribution Network
gyanbooks.com
India, USA, Canada, UK, Australia

ISBN: 978-93-7014-306-7 (PB)

First Published, 1915

2nd Impression 2025

Printed at: Gyan Press, Delhi.

PROMOTION OF LEARNING IN INDIA
Author: NARENDRA NATH LAW, WALTER K. FIRMINGER

PROMOTION OF LEARNING IN INDIA

BY EARLY EUROPEAN SETTLERS

(UP TO ABOUT 1800 A.D.)

PROMOTION OF LEARNING IN INDIA

BY EARLY EUROPEAN SETTLERS

(UP TO ABOUT 1800 A.D.)

BY

NARENDRA NATH LAW, M.A., B.L.

AUTHOR OF "STUDIES IN ANCIENT HINDU POLITY," ETC.

WITH AN INTRODUCTION

BY THE

VEN. WALTER K. FIRMINGER, M.A., B.D.

ARCHDEACON OF CALCUTTA

PRESIDENT CALCUTTA HISTORICAL SOCIETY

WITH 2 ILLUSTRATIONS

LONGMANS, GREEN AND CO

39 PATERNOSTER ROW, LONDON

FOURTH AVENUE AND 30TH STREET, NEW YORK

BOMBAY, CALCUTTA, AND MADRAS

1915

TO THE MEMORY
OF
MY REVERED
MOTHER

PREFACE.

THE efforts of the Europeans in India for diffusion of education in their own community as well as among the people of this country before the nineteenth century are worthy of record. Such efforts, no doubt, were prompted by considerations of religious propagandism but did not obscure a genuine desire to spread the blessings of education on its own account.

Education though left in abeyance at first formed, later on, the object of solicitude not merely of the European missionaries but also of the European merchants and officials both here and in Europe. The zeal evinced by some of them can well stand a comparison with that of their illustrious successors such as Hare and Bethune, though in point of accomplished works, the former may rank lower owing to the uncongenial soil upon which their pioneering labours were spent. An attempt has been made in this volume to give a connected narrative of the educational efforts of these enthusiastic pioneers of European education and their fellow-workers.

I have to express my heart-felt thanks to Prof. Radhakumud Mookerji, M.A., author of *A History of Indian Shipping*, etc., and Mr. H. Beveridge, I.C.S. (retired), for their kind revision of the work; Prof. Benoy Kumar Sarkar, M.A., author of *The Positive Background of Hindu Sociology*, etc., for his suggestions about the arrangement of the matter of the book; my uncle, Mr. Nundolal Dey, M.A., B.L., author of *The Geographical Dictionary of Ancient and Mediæval India*, etc., Mr. Balailal Dutt, B.A., Librarian, A.S.B., Mr. S. R. Dass, bar.-at-law, Mr. H. K. Basu, bar.-at-law, Mr. Narasinha Chandra Pal, and my cousins, Messrs. Nalin Chandra Paul, B.L., and Satya Churn Law, M.A., B.L., for help of various kinds.

NARENDRA NATH LAW.

96, Amherst Street,
Calcutta.
September, 1915.

INTRODUCTION.

In the present volume of his *Promotion of Learning in India*, my friend, Mr. Narendra Nath Law, deals with the very interesting subject of the efforts made by Europeans in India to provide the machinery of public instruction. Those of Mr. Law's readers who may think that the efforts described are of a somewhat meagre and unsatisfactory nature, might well be asked to bear in mind three important facts:—

(1) In the year 1818 it is calculated that in England "for one child who had the opportunity of education, three were left entirely ignorant," and we are told, by way of illustration of the lamentable state of things then existing, that the prosperous town of Preston, "one of the

richest cities in the great manufacturing county of Lancaster, with a population of 18,000 persons, had an endowed school, educating only thirty-six children." There were three other schools in the town, one taught by a master, and two by mistresses, but it is not known how many children shared the doubtful advantages of these miserable institutions. It has been observed that there are some things which all men profess to admire *in the abstract*, but which they detest *in the concrete*, and that in the eighteenth and early part of the nineteenth century, public instruction was one of the most marked of those things. The observation, however, fails to do justice to facts. The truth is that during the period which falls under review in the present work, the average man maintained that ignorance is a positive blessing to the poor, and that to instruct the children of the poor is, in the long run, only to make the poor discontented with a lot which it is neither desirable nor indeed possible to alter.

(2) In the year of grace, 1914, if the old prejudices are less vigorous than they were, the importance of the cause of public instruction is even yet insufficiently understood. The most convincing evidence for this assertion is afforded by the place which the schoolmaster holds in the esteem of the community. There are, of course, the few who can find their way to well-paid appointments in the most expensive of our public schools, and it is true that the rapid advance towards efficiency which has been made by the State Provided Schools has led to a certain improvement in the lot of those who impart instruction to the children of the poor. Yet, is it not still the case, that "schooling" is one of the last resources of the graduate, too old to enter the Army, not smart enough for the Bar, not "good" enough for the Civil Service, or "pious" enough to enter Holy Orders?

It may be that parents belonging to the upper middle classes cannot afford to pay enough to secure a really sound education for their children, but whatever may be the cause, the result is to be found in the existence of "*crammers*," "*corresponding colleges*," and the like. We are still quite content with those respectable minor schools, which, after having had our children entrusted to their care for five or six years, send them out not able to write three lines of a dead language without making a blunder, or speak for one minute in a modern language and be understood. It may be true that our poverty compels us to endure a state of things which it would cost much money to remedy, but the salient fact is that on the whole our people love to have things so. It is now fairly widely realised that the would-be teacher has to be taught to teach; but if teaching is a profession which requires a considerable outlay in securing the necessary qualifications, the returns for the outlay are usually miserably small. India, at the present time, offers no career to the competent schoolmaster; in this country his salary is inadequate, and his prospects in his own profession are almost nil.

(3) In judging, then, the efforts made in the past, we need to be reminded that enthusiasm for public instruction, outside the ranks of those who have powerful religious motives for taking up the work, is not of very ancient *provenance.* It is well when we read of the alleged corruption of the Civil Service in the days of Clive and his immediate successors, to read some such work as Trevelyan's *Early History of Charles James Fox*, and compare what we read of morals in Bengal with what we read of morals in England. It is well, in like manner, to compare the state of feeling in regard to the importance of education in England in 1715–1815, with the state of feeling in India during the same

period. It is well to measure our own efforts before we slight those of our predecessors.

Mr. Law is occupied in the present volume mainly with the subject of European endeavours to educate the young. He, however, touches upon the more general subject of learning in India when he deals with the origin of the Asiatic Society of Bengal. It is to be hoped that in a future volume the author will take up the fascinating subject of the early pioneers in European studies of Asiatic thought. The subject is a very wide one and also very deep, and the difficulty increases when we remember that meagre and jejune as the lucubrations of Holwell on Oriental subjects may appear at the present day, yet in their own time, they represented a real advance in knowledge.

In the course of a study of the old records, I have come across several interesting evidences of ancient workers in the rich mine of Oriental learning: but I have never had leisure to follow the subject up. Here is an example: On November 17th, 1783, Col. Henry Watson writes to recommend to the notice of Government Mr. Reuben Burrow[1]; to the qualifications of his *protégé* the Colonel adds, "*In the first instance, from no other information than the Bramin precession of the Equinox, he has determined those periods of the Hindoos called the four Jogues, which have been so often mentioned by ancient and modern authors, and cause such numerous mistakes and conjectures among the learned. He has proved these Jogues to be nothing more than astronomical periods, and has deduced from them their original periods; but what is still more extraordinary and curious, he has found that they clearly explain some very ancient chronological cycles that were mentioned by Beerosus, a Chaldean author*

[1] See the article on Reuben Burrow in the *Dictionary of National Biography.*

(who lived about two thousand years ago) which caused many disputes and controversies among the European philosophers.

"He has also discovered that several branches of science which were supposed to be the invention of Europeans, were long since known to the Bramins; that they were acquainted with decimals and algebraic computation, and also, that they had determined the mean motions of the Sun and Moon and several other parts of astronomy to almost as great exactness four thousand years ago as the Europeans have done in the present age. By an ancient astronomical table made when the obliquity of the Ecliptic was twenty-four degrees two minutes, Mr. Burrow was able to draw the foregoing conclusion, as the variation is determined to be nearly half a second in a year, which almost proves the table to have been made at least four thousand years ago. He is further of opinion, from what he has already seen, that the ancient Bramins did possess several

improvements in science that the moderns may be entirely unacquainted with, and, therefore, concludes that an enquiry after their knowledge may lead to matters of the first importance.

"*From the above-mentioned discoveries made in a few weeks by Mr. Burrow, I am led to believe that many other lights into ancient learning of India will soon be made, and which may be of much greater consequence and value than can at present be foreseen; I am also of opinion that the desire to become acquainted with Hindoo learning will be increased among the Company's servants in proportion as the knowledge of the discoveries are made known to the public. In this enlightened age, when every nation endeavours to establish its title and claim to new discoveries, what I have already said of the capacity and zeal for acquirement of knowledge, so remarkable in Mr. Burrow, will, I flatter myself, be sufficient to entitle him to the patronage of the Board, even when his abilities to be useful to the Corps of Engineers are out of question.*"

This extract is but one of the many which might be given to show that there is a wealth of material to hand for the treatment of the subject I have indicated. Of Hastings' interest in Eastern lore much has been written, but the matter has never been adequately dealt with. There is again the subject of the influence of the early publications of the Asiatic Society of Bengal on contemporary European thought. Here again I must content myself with a single striking illustration. Monsieur C. Latreille, in his extremely valuable work, *Joseph de Maistre et la Papauté*, writes: "*Il avait suivi avec infiniment d'intérêt les publications de la Société Asiatique de Calcutta et ses principaux membres, William Jones, son fondateur, Bentley et Claudius Buchanan. Cette Société, créé en* 1784, *pénétra dans le sanctuaire de la religion et dans les archives des adorateurs de Brahmah: elle fit des découvertes aussi utiles à la science qu'au Christianisme. Ses mémoires imprimés à Calcutta et réimprimes à Londres*[1] *étaient lus assidument par J. de Maistre, qui, signalant les utiles travaux de l'Académie de Calcutta, dira des les Soirées que 'l'Europe doit des actions de grâce à cette société anglaise.'*" An analysis of the authorities on Indian subjects quoted by F. de la Mennais in his *Essai sur l'indifférence en Matière de Religion* might perhaps yield some interesting results.

Professor Rhys Davids in the preface to his *Buddhist India* has employed some rather bitter language in his description of the conditions under which a British student of Indian history, law, or languages is usually compelled to do his work. A survey of the encouragement given by the English and German universities to the study of Sanskrit might

[1] Two volumes of the Society's Proceedings appeared in French in 1809 with notes by Delambre, de Cuvier, and de Langlès.

suggest the idea that India is a part, not of the English but the German Empire. Under the conditions that have prevailed until the present time, the man who has the rare capacity to deal with Oriental learning is compelled to spend all the best hours of his working day in teaching the young, and in most cases it is probably true that the man who is possessed of the necessary gifts for research work has but the slightest ability to impart elementary instruction. This is the burden of Dr. Rhys Davids' complaint and when we turn from England to India, we are all the more struck with wonder that so much has been achieved for Indian studies by men who have only been able to give to them the fag-end of a heavy working day. It has, I believe, been no small amount of weakness in the British administration that work which should have been made a first charge on those competent to do it has been regarded as a mere πάρεργον, and that labours which should be the first care of a genuinely civilised Government have been left to the mere haphazard of casual volunteers. Science not only requires the encouragement of the civilized State, but the State should see to it that the results of learned research should be made available in a form which the public can understand. In the belief that Mr. Law's survey of the *Promotion of Learning in India* will further the greater end which all true learning has in view, I have ventured to write this brief Introduction to the present volume.

WALTER K. FIRMINGER.

ST. JOHN'S HOUSE,
CALCUTTA.
Xmas Eve, 1914.

TABLE OF CONTENTS.

BOOK I.

SOUTHERN INDIA.

CHAPTER I.

EDUCATIONAL ACTIVITY UNDER ENGLISH E. I. CO.

CHAPTER IV.

CHAPTER V.

BOOK II.

NORTHERN INDIA.

CHAPTER I.

CALCUTTA AND ITS VICINITY.

CHAPTER II.

ILLUSTRATIONS.

BOOK I.

SOUTHERN INDIA.

Prelimi-
nary.

PRELIMINARY.

THE efforts of Muslim monarchs, chiefs and private individuals during Islamic rule in India for the promotion of learning have been noticed elsewhere.[1] Such laudable exertions were not, however, confined to them alone. The different European peoples that began to land in India since the sixteenth century or earlier were not altogether inactive in regard to diffusion of education and learning not only among themselves but also among the people of this country. The early history of such efforts on their part is very obscure, which makes it difficult to write a connected account of activities in this direction of all the sections of Europeans

[1] See *Promotion of Learning in India during Muhammadan Rule (by Muhammadans)*, by the same author.

that began to come to India since the time of the earlier Mughal emperors. We shall, however, try to give a connected narrative of such efforts so far as may be gleaned from the materials at our command.

Religious Education.

CHAPTER I.

EDUCATIONAL ACTIVITY UNDER ENGLISH E. I. CO. IN SOUTHERN INDIA.

SECTION I.

Religious Education.

IN the early history of the East India Company it would be futile to search for evidences of any direct efforts on their part for promotion of learning among the people of India or even among the Europeans born in this place. It should be borne in mind that the first efforts of the Company to diffuse education were prompted by a religious motive, viz. the evangelization of Indians and the removal of apprehended trouble owing to the preponderance of Roman Catholics among the inhabitants of the places where they had settled. Says Mr. J. W. Kaye on

Chapter I. Sect. I.

Religious Education.

this point: "Sleeman had established schools of industry at Jabbulpore for the children of the Thugs, Outram had put to school in Khandesh the little Bhils whose fathers he had reclaimed, and MacPherson had turned to similar account his opportunities in favour of the victims whom he had rescued from the hands of the sacrificing Khonds. Education of the people in any substantial shape begins within a comparatively recent period. There is recognition, in some of the early charters, of the Christian duty of instructing the Gentoos, but it was not until 1813 that there was anything like a decided manifestation of the will of Government in connexion with the great subject."[1]

The very early educational efforts of the Europeans, as I have already indicated, had an ulterior purpose, viz. the propagation of the Gospel. Moreover, they were

[1] J. W. Kaye's *Administration of the E. I. Co.*, Pt. V., Ch. I., p. 587.

Religious Education.

directed purely to religious education—the objects being the instillation of Christian doctrines into the minds of the people through their native language which the Europeans tried to master, as also the spread of Western education among the Indians in order to enable them to appreciate better the Christian doctrines. As early as 1614 A.D., we hear of steps being taken for the recruitment of Indians for the propagation of the Gospel among their countrymen and for imparting to these missionaries such education at the Company's expense as would enable them to carry out effectively the purposes for which they were enlisted. Captain Best took home an Indian youth, christened him Peter,—a name that was chosen by the King himself (James I.),—and educated him at the Company's expense in order to give him a suitable outfit for his task. The youth got a decent education; but as to what he did in furtherance of the evangelical purpose, nothing is

Chapter I. Sect. I.

Religious Education.

known.[1] The movement for the proselytization of India was going on, and many schemes were put forward. The Hon. Robert Boyle, the philosopher, re-opened in 1677 the question originated by Baxter in 1660, by recommending to the East India Company, of which he himself was a Director, a plan of his own. The essence of the plan was to make use of the Company's Chaplains as missionaries by giving them a special training for the purpose. Dr. Fell, Bishop of Oxford, undertook to train men in the knowledge of Arabic, if the Company would send students to Oxford and bear the cost of their training. The means at the disposal of the projectors to carry out their plan were:—

(1) They had Boyle's translation of the Gospel and the Acts of the Apostles in *Malay* (*i.e.* Malayālam or Tamil).

[1] Rev. Frank Penny's *Church in Madras*, Vol. I., pp. 14–16.

(2) They had Pocock's translation of Grotius' *Truth of the Christian Religion* in Arabic.

(3) There was the teaching afforded by the Professorship of Arabic, established at Oxford by Archbishop Laud in 1636.

(4) There was Bishop Fell's offer to superintend the training of the youths in Arabic.

(5) They looked to the liberal financial assistance of the members of the East India Company.

This scheme, however, failed for various reasons, such as Bishop Fell's death in 1686, the lapse of the Company's Charter in 1693 and its renewal for only five years. Arabic and "Malaian" were, moreover, found out to be ineffective media for the evangelization of India. A part of the funds that had been raised for the purpose was therefore spent over printing and distributing Boyle's Malay version of the Gospel in the Company's settlements,[1]

[1] *Penny*, Vol. I., pp. 95–98.

the rest being returned to the subscribers. Some time after, the Company thought that books in Portuguese would be more effective, and made liberal gifts of such books for distribution among the people in the Company's settlements.[1] But herein also the Company missed the mark. The Portuguese *lingua franca* of the European settlements in India was a *patois*-combination of several languages, of which pure Portuguese was but a framework. Books in pure Portuguese were as unintelligible to them as English. To meet this difficulty, Mr. Lewis, the Company's chaplain at Fort St. George (1691–1714), studied and soon became proficient in the *patois*, in which he continued for a while to impart religious instruction to the people. But with his departure, the Portuguese *patois* fell out of favour and his successors gave more attention to education through English.[2]

[1] *Penny*, Vol. I., pp. 95–98. [2] *Ibid.*, p. 113.

SECTION II.

Secular Education.

Secular Education. Portuguese Medium.

While describing the steps taken by the Company to propagate religious education among the people through Arabic, Tamil, etc., and to train men for the work, I should not omit to give an account of what the Company and the Missionaries did for the secular education of the people.

(a) *Portuguese Medium.*

In 1670 the Directors made inquiries about the education of the children at Fort St. George, and expressed themselves very strongly as to how they ought to be brought up. In 1673 action was taken by the appointment of a Scotch preacher named Pringle who kept a school for teaching the Portuguese Eurasians, British Eurasians, and the children of a few Indian subordinates

Chapter I. Sect. II.

Portuguese Medium.

for whom the Company considered themselves responsible, the medium of teaching being the debased kind of Portuguese already referred to. His salary was £50 a year. On Mr. Pringle's return to England, Mr. Ralph Ord was appointed to the vacant post on the same salary. He carried on tuition at the Fort for four years from 1678, and was allowed, unlike his predecessor, to do other work as well. In 1682 he retired on account of ill-health, Mr. John Barker being chosen as his successor on a salary of 6 *pagodas* per mensem, *i.e.* half of what his predecessors had enjoyed. This arrangement, it seems, lasted up to 1707, when Barker died. This small school grew in importance and attracted towards it gradually-increasing charity-stock for the care and education of the orphans,[1] making a thorough supervision of the institution a matter of

[1] *Penny*, Vol. I., pp. 164–166; also *Vestiges of Old Madras*, by H. D. Love, Vol. I., p. 397, and Vol. II., pp. 163 ff.

Portuguese Medium.

necessity. Such supervision carved a good deal out of the almost independent position enjoyed by Barker in the first few years of his career as schoolmaster. After 1692 the work of superintendence was entrusted by the Directors to the Chaplains, who were required to have a knowledge of Portuguese and Tamil for the performance of their new duty. Mr. Lewis, to whom we have already referred in another connexion, was an enthusiastic educationist, and recommended to Mr. Pitt, Governor of the Fort (1698–1709), the foundation of two *Nurseries*, one for boys and the other for girls, where they should be educated and taught the Protestant religion. Lewis' object was to make Portuguese the medium of instruction. He had both Prayer-books and Catechism in that language, and himself commenced the translation of portions of the Bible. But his plan was not carried out. His translation, however, was not so much labour lost. He sent his manuscript to Ziegenbalg and Grundler, the Danish missionaries at Tranquebar, who were induced thereby to translate the whole Bible. It was copies of this translation that they distributed among the students of the Portuguese schools they established afterwards at Tranquebar, Fort St. David, and Madras. Though Lewis' scheme was not adopted by the Company and a different line was followed, yet it must be said to his credit that his zeal in this matter had prompted him to do what lay in his power to promote the cause of education.[1] He himself, without waiting for any help from the Company or any other source, had founded a free school, which was carried on by himself as long as he remained in the Fort, and for a short time after his departure, by his successor the Rev. William Stevenson. The traveller Lockyer, who visited the Fort

[1] *Penny*, Vol. I., pp. 166-167.

Chapter I. Sect. II. — English Medium: St. Mary's School.

in 1703, has left an account[1] of the place as it was in Lewis' time, which reflects much credit on Lewis. He says that the free school was held in a large room under the Church Library which, by the way, was not a meagre collection, containing, as it did, books valued at £438.[2]

(b) *English Medium: St. Mary's School.*

Lewis' successor Stevenson did not like this institution, and thought that an English school for the children of English soldiers would be more useful than a Portuguese school. So he established an English school (St. Mary's) and left the Portuguese teaching to the Danish missionaries.[3]

Lewis' institution and scheme did not recommend themselves to the local

[1] Lockyer's *Account of Trade in India.*

[2] *Penny,* Vol. I., pp. 131–133.

[3] *Ibid.,* p. 167; also H. D. Love's *V.O.M.,* Vol. II., p. 164.

Chapter I. Sect. II.

St. Mary's School.

authorities at the Fort for three reasons:—

(i) They did not know Portuguese, in which Lewis had been proficient; (ii) the Society for Promoting Christian Knowledge had already materially assisted the Danish missionaries with funds for the establishment of schools in which the medium of instruction was Portuguese; and (iii) funds being small, attention to British Eurasians exclusively and an English school for them could alone be admitted.[1]

Stevenson, however, was in favour of founding another school for the Proselytes, but this plan was not carried out. The English school alone was founded and opened in December, 1715, with 18 boys and 12 girls, under the name of St. Mary's Charity School. Among the boys was a Portuguese youth sent by Mr. Grundler, the Danish missionary at Tranquebar, at the recommendation of

[1] *Penny*, Vol. I., p. 167.

the S.P.C.K.,[1] to study English at the school, in order that he might be of help to the mission of the Society.[2]

(i) *Renewal of Charter—a Fillip to Education and leading to the Foundation of St. Mary's School.*

It should be remarked here that at the time of the renewal of the Charter towards the end of the seventeenth century, many criticisms were passed upon the doings of the Company. The report written in 1695 by Dr. Prideaux, Dean of Norwich, contained for instance an adverse remark which, it must be admitted, had some truth in it. "The Dutch," says he, "had lately erected a college or university in Ceylon. . . . The English East India Company are in this matter

[1] The Society for Promoting Christian Knowledge was founded in 1698, and the Society for the Propagation of the Gospel incorporated by Royal Charter in 1701. *Vide* W. W. Hunter's *India of the Queen*, pp. 231, 232.

[2] *Penny*, Vol. I., pp. 168, 169.

negligent." He put forward a scheme of his own, which among other things included a recommendation for the erection of schools at Madras, Bombay, and Fort St. David for the education of the inhabitants. Prideaux's scheme was not followed *in toto*, but the effect of his remark and the like criticisms from other quarters was that an express provision was put in the New Charter for ensuring greater care for the instruction of the people.[1] The Company had no doubt appointed schoolmasters for teaching the European and Eurasian youths of the Fort settlement, but could not reply to the charge that they paid little attention to the Indians under their care. The charter therefore made the following provision :—

"*All Ministers shall be obliged to learn*

---

1 *Penny*, Vol. I., p. 122; also Anderson's *History of the Colonial Church*, Vol. II., pp. 704, 708.

within one year after their arrival the Portuguese language and shall apply themselves to learn the native language of the country where they shall reside, the better to enable them to instruct the Gentoos that shall be the servants or the slaves of the Company, or of their agents, in the Protestant Religion.

"*We further will and direct that the Company shall provide schoolmasters in all the said garrisons and superior factories where they shall be found necessary.*"[1] Another provision in the charter was that "*schoolmasters shall be attached to every ship over 500 tons burthen.*"[2]

The emphasis laid by the Directors on the necessity of education of the people under Company's care acted no doubt as a fillip to the local authorities; and the establishment of St. Mary's Charity School was one of the results of the greater attention paid to the matter by the authorities in England.

[1] *Penny*, Vol. I., p. 123; *vide* also Kaye's *Administration of the E. I. Co.* (1853), p. 626.

[2] *Penny*, Vol. I., p. 346.

St. Mary's School: Rules.

(ii) *Rules of St. Mary's School, showing its Internal Arrangement.*

The Rules of this Charity School as recorded by Mr. Wheeler[1] throw much light on its internal state, and so, I think, no apology is necessary for quoting them here :—

"1. *That in some convenient place within the English Town, there be proper accommodation made at first for 30 poor Protestant children, diet and education gratis.*

"2. *That the scholars be trained up to a practical sense of religion and be particularly instructed in the doctrines of the Church of England as by law established; and therefore, no person shall be capable of being master of the school unless he be qualified according to the Acts of Parliament.*

"3. *That the children, whether boys or girls, shall be taken into the school house at 5 years of age, or thereabouts, and be put out to service or apprenticeships when they are about 12 years old. And while they are entertained in the school, the boys shall be taught to read, write,*

[1] Wheeler's *Madras in the Olden Time*, pp. 341, 342 (ed. 1882).

St. Mary's School: Rules.

cast accounts, or what they may be further capable of, and the girls shall be instructed in reading and the necessary parts of housewifery.

"4. *That no scholar shall be taken in, nor any matter of moment transacted without the previous consent of the Honourable Governor for the time being.*

"5. *That besides the Ministers and Churchwardens, who shall always be overseers of the Charity School, there be three others chosen yearly by the vestry for the better management and more careful inspection of the affairs of the school; and in order thereunto, that the said overseers (or at least four of them) meet every week at the vestry, and keep minutes of what they agree upon (if it be of any moment) to be laid before the Governor for his approbation.*

"6. *That one of the overseers annually chosen by the vestry shall at the same time be nominated Treasurer to the School, and be obliged to keep exact regular accounts of the school-stock and expenses, to be laid before every vestry, and before the other overseers, or any of the contributors, when they require it, at any of their weekly meetings or otherwise.*

"7. *That when the cash belonging to the school-stock shall amount to the sum of* 1000 *pagodas, it shall be employed at sea, or let out at interest, by the Treasurer, with the advice of the rest of the overseers, and the consent of the Governor;*

and if the money cannot be thus employed, that it be lent to the Church at the usual interest.

"8. *That all Bonds, Deeds of Conveyance and other writs for the use and benefit of the Charity School, shall be drawn and granted in the name of the Treasurer and other overseers for the time being.*

"9. *That all Legacies, Gifts and Benefactions to the school, whether of money or other things, be duly entered by the Treasurer in a book to be kept for that purpose, which he shall sign at the foot of every page.*

"10. *That no part of the school-stock shall on any pretence whatsoever be employed to any purpose, or in any other manner, but what is agreeable to the original design and institution above expressed.*

"11. *That in all difficult cases and disputes about any matter of consequence, the overseers shall make application to the Governor for calling a vestry, wherein all such matters shall be determined by the majority of the contributors.*

"12. *That the aforesaid articles shall be the standing rules and fundamental constitutions of the Charity School, according to which the overseers shall be obliged to act. And therefore that the said rules shall be registered in the beginning of a book, wherein the said overseers shall enter all the subsequent orders and regulations which they may have occasion to make hereafter concerning the said school,*

St. Mary's School: Initial Stages.

provided that such subsequent orders shall be first approved by the Governor and Council for the time being."

The chief points to be noticed about these rules are that the school was to be a Church of England school; that it was to be managed by a body of seven persons —2 Ministers, 2 Churchwardens, and 3 Overseers elected by the vestry; and that in matters of importance, *e.g.* admission of children, the Governor in Council must be consulted.

(iii) *Initial Stages.*

Some time after the foundation of the school, there were in it more than 30 children. Over and above the endowed funds, a monthly collection was made for their education and maintenance. The boys lived in one apartment under the charge of a master and an usher, and the girls in a separate house under the care of a mistress and an assistant.[1]

[1] *Penny*, Vol. I., pp. 171–175.

Chapter I. Sect. II.

St. Mary's School: Teachers and School Sites.

The school opened with about £350 bequeathed to it by two legacies, but the sum within a short time amounted to £1000 by additional contributions, the Governor himself paying £225. At first for the purposes of the school, hired buildings were used; but in 1717, the Jearsey House and ground were made over to the school by the Company. Liberal gifts of Primers, Spelling Books, Bibles and Catechisms were also made.[1] The school authorities, however, decided to erect a new building on the Island in the river on the west side of the Fort, out of the sale-proceeds of the Jearsey House and ground. The school began to use this new building from 1719 till the construction of stronger and more scientific defence works of the Fort in 1746 for resisting attacks by the French made it necessary to remove elsewhere.[2]

The outlay for the new building was

[1] *Penny*, Vol. I., pp. 171–175.

[2] *Ibid.*, pp. 174–176.

5000 *pagodas*. The authorities were not cramped for room in the Island. We learn from the appreciative opinion of the Governor and Council that "it was substantial and an ornament to the place."[1]

(iv) *Roll of Teachers and Changes of School Site.*

John Mitchel was the first schoolmaster of St. Mary's School. But within six months of his appointment he was prosecuted in the Mayor's Court by the commandant of the Garrison for deluding his daughter by a pretended marriage in which he acted both as priest and husband. Mitchel had pretended to be in Holy Orders though he was a soldier, and the authorities had accepted his statement and acted accordingly. He was called upon to find sureties for good behaviour and ordered to leave for England at the earliest opportunity. It was indeed very

[1] *Penny*, Vol. I., pp. 174–176.

Chapter I. Sect. II.

St. Mary's School: Teachers and School Sites.

unfortunate that such an incident should take place in the infancy of the school.[1] Mitchel was dismissed and Main was appointed in his place.

When necessity arose for the school to give up the site in the Island in 1746, the compensation it obtained from the Company was somewhat short of what it ought to have been paid; but the Company was hard up now, and the school authorities had no other alternative than to accept the low compensation. The Company, however, made partial amends by accepting a loan of 3000 *pagodas* from the School Funds at a temporary high rate of interest.

After its removal from the Island, the school was lodged in two separate houses—one bought and the other hired. Shortly after, the Trustees sold to the Government for 300 *pagodas* the site of the school they had bought. Three months later, the Fort and the walled

[1] *Penny*, Vol. I., pp. 174–176.

Chapter I. Sect. II.

St. Mary's School: Teachers and School Sites.

town of Madraspatam (Madras) were occupied by the French.[1]

Mr. Samuel Staveley, who had been in 1742 a schoolmaster in the Whitgift Free School of England, offered in 1753 to keep and superintend the Charity School, provided he obtained an extra salary of £100. The offer was accepted, and one of the houses in Middle Gate Street bequeathed by Mrs. Mary Williams to the vestry was used for the purpose. The school thus brought inside the Fort continued there until 1872. The vestry and the people generally were much satisfied with this arrangement and proposed to the gentlemen of Fort St. David to amalgamate the Charity-stock there with the Charity-stock of Fort St. George and to educate the children of the military of both the places under Mr. Staveley. It seems that the proposal was accepted.[2] The school, however, met with a crisis

[1] *Penny*, Vol. I., pp. 176–179.

[2] *Ibid.*, p. 314.

St. Mary's School: Teachers and School Sites.

during the siege of 1758–59. The building in which it was lodged was destroyed by shot and shell, in consequence of which it had to remove to a house lent by the Company. In 1778 it wanted repair, for which, as also for taking in more orphan-children of the soldiers of the Company, greater funds were needed.

The vestry resolved to raise a subscription at the Presidency and the different subordinate stations, but the resolution failed on account of the unfavourable time then prevailing owing to wars. In 1779 the bad condition of the school-house necessitated the removal of the children to the Church lodgings for a time. Another house was applied for from the Company, which, however, could not comply with the request. In the meantime, a house was hired at the rent of 60 *pagodas* a month, which the school could only pay with the greatest difficulty. The vestry now proposed to Government to

St. Mary's School: Teachers and School Sites.

repair and alter the old school building at its own expense (the cost being 785 *pagodas*), and asked for either a gift of the house or a lease for 99 years of the ground in Middle Gate Street at a quit rent. The latter request was granted, and the lease was sanctioned at the rent of 5 *pagodas* per annum. The vestry then put the building in repair and continued to use it for its purpose.[1] In 1785, however, the renewed building collapsed, and Colonel Patrick Ross, the Chief Engineer, gave an estimate for rebuilding, amounting to 2300 *pagodas*. The plan was sanctioned and arrangements were made for the carrying on of the school in a rented house in Black Town.[2] Government was appealed to for financial help and in response it paid 500 *pagodas*. By the end of the year, the building was

[1] *Penny*, Vol. I., pp. 361-362; *V.O.M.*, Vol. III., p. 349.

[2] The place outside the Fort or White Town was so called. It was inhabited by Indians.

Chapter I. Sect. II.

St. Mary's School: Finances.

completed and became fit for being used for the school.[1]

(v) *Finances.*

We have already mentioned some of the methods by which the funds for the school were raised. An additional but unusual method was as follows:—

The "Choultry Dubash" (interpreter) was tried by the Council for extorting exorbitant fees from poor people. He was dismissed from service, pilloried and fined 500 *pagodas*, one half of which was paid to the school.[2]

Another source of income of the school was that "all boats (of the place where the school was) that were employed of a Sunday used to pay 6 *fanams* every trip to the school-stock."[3]

It may not be out of place to record

[1] *Penny,* Vol. I., pp. 382–384; *V.O.M.*, Vol. III., p. 350.

[2] *Ibid.*, p. 176.

[3] *Ibid.*, p. 314.

here a few legacies out of which the school derived benefit. In 1720, Charles Davis died and left a legacy of 200 *pagodas*.[1] Some of the legacies bequeathed to the institution in the second half of the eighteenth century were [2]—

1. Nicholas Morse, formerly governor . . . . 800 *pagodas*
2. Col. John Wood, the designer of Christ Church, Trichinoply . 200 „
3. Robert Hughes . . . . 180 „
4. Mrs. Isabella Croke . . . . . 150 „
5. James Stringer . . . . 240 „

Such legacies are a good index of the confidence that the community placed in the efficient management of the school. Larger legacies than those recorded above were at times left by Europeans to meet the educational wants of the European settlements. James Wooley, for instance, left a very large sum of money for the education and provision of the distressed European children. This legacy, it is

[1] *Penny*, Vol. I., p. 176.
[2] *Ibid.*, pp. 399.

interesting to note, is associated with Mr. John Balfour, the great-grandfather of the two distinguished statesmen of England of the present day.[1] He was one of the executors of Mr. Wooley. The European children in various schools in the Madras Presidency, including those of the Roman Catholic persuasion, still enjoy the benefit of the legacy.[2]

(vi) *Part played by the Company in Educational Matters in the Seventeenth and Eighteenth Centuries.*

We are now in a position to judge of the nature of help given to the school by the Company and the local Government. The idea of a free mission school for the children of the Portuguese and others originated with the S.P.C.K. in London. Their intention was to carry it out by the Danish missionaries. Mr. Lewis fell in with the idea and discussed it with

[1] *Penny*, Vol. I., pp. 399, 400.
[2] *Ibid.*, p. 400.

E. I. Company's part in Educational Matters.

Ziegenbalg, a Danish missionary of Tranquebar in 1710. Stevenson, his successor, gave effect to a fresh scheme[1] which provided for a school for the British Eurasians. The Company gave a site for the school but had nothing to do with the building or its up-keep. They intervened to safeguard the funds and their proper administration. When the surrender of the Fort to the French put the funds in danger, they stepped in for their safe custody.[2]

In the seventeenth century we find the Directors taking the initiative in educational work, but with the arrival of the missionaries in the beginning of the eighteenth century we find a change gradually setting in. They shifted their educational duties to the shoulders of the new-comers, though of course they did not stand aloof altogether. During the first three quarters of the eighteenth century

1 *Penny*, Vol. I., pp. 176–179.
2 *Ibid.*

Chapter I. Sect. II.

E. I. Company's part in Educational Matters.

they gave assistance to schools of various kinds in various ways; they ordered, for instance, their servants at Fort St. David to act in the schools as accountants, and occasionally repaired the school buildings. They did not, however, want to have a hand in the actual educational work, so that, up to 1787, all that was done outside Fort St. George was done by the missionaries either in their capacity as such, or as garrison or station chaplains.[1]

[1] *Penny*, Vol. I., p. 505.

CHAPTER II.

EDUCATIONAL ACTIVITY OUTSIDE FORT ST. GEORGE.

(a) *Schwartz.*

LET us for a while look at the educational work that was being done outside Fort St. George. The S.P.C.K. missionaries were one and all graduates of universities and zealous educationists. None of them worked without schools. Schwartz, a German missionary,[1] established the vestry school for European and Eurasian boys at Trichinopoly (about 1772 A.D.). The events that led to the foundation of the institution were very sad.[2] In 1772, January 14, a powder magazine blew up; 34 European soldiers and 10 Sepoys were

[1] Sent out first by the Danes, but afterwards engaged in English missions.

[2] *Penny*, Vol. I., p. 505.

killed, and 66 Europeans and 44 Sepoys wounded. They left behind both widows and children. Schwartz moved in the matter, and had no difficulty in raising a sufficient sum among the civil officials and soldiers of all grades in the garrison to pay a non-commissioned officer and his wife to look after the orphans and instruct them. Thus originated the *vestry school at Trichinopoly.*[1]

Schwartz soon founded another school at Tanjore. The circumstances that led to its foundation were as follows:—In 1774 he went to Tanjore and made it his headquarters. Thence he was requested by the Governor to come to Fort St. George in the same year and commissioned to bear despatches to Ḥaidar 'Alī of Mysore. Ḥaidar presented him with a bag of money for the expenses of his journey which Schwartz declined, as the expenses were to be paid by the Madras Government. Ḥaidar would

[1] *Penny*, Vol. I., pp. 505, 506.

take no refusal, and so the bag was accepted; but on his return, Schwartz delivered it to Governor and Council, who again urged him to take it. Whereupon he took permission to employ the sum as the nucleus fund for founding an English Charity School at Tanjore, expressing a hope that the fund would increase by contributions from charitable people.[1] Thus originated the *Tanjore English Charity School.*

(b) *Other Educationists.*

We learn from the S.P.C.K. *Reports* as well as Taylor's *Memoir*[2] as quoted in *Penny* that there was *a school at Vepery*, a village on the Coromandel Coast, where Benjamin Johnson, "English and Portuguese School master and clerk to the Portuguese congregation," died in 1773. There were also at this time *two English schools for Eurasians of both*

[1] *Penny*, Vol. I., pp. 505, 506.
[2] Taylor's *Memoir*, p. 33.

Chapter II.

A Roman Catholic School managed by Capuchin Missionaries.

sexes, one at Vepery and another at Cuddalore. These schools owed their being, not to the Company, but to the Missionaries of the S.P.C.K., nor were they regularly assisted by the Madras Government. Moreover, they were all managed by the Missionaries. With the exception of the St. Mary's Charity School, the Company now took no part in the management of the schools.[1]

(c) *A Roman Catholic School managed by Capuchin Missionaries.*

In Black Town (as the place, outside the Fort or White Town, inhabited by Indians was called) *a Roman Catholic School* was established under the management of Capuchin missionaries, providing for the education of Europeans and Eurasians along with boys from other communities.[2] This school was more

[1] *Penny,* Vol. I., pp. 506, 507.
[2] *Ibid.*

A Roman Catholic School managed by Capuchin Mission-aries.

largely endowed than any other hitherto established and had no other connexion with the Company than that of benevolent protection. This institution supplemented in a large measure the works of the existing educational foundations.

Chapter III. Sect. I.

Lady Campbell's Female Orphan Asylum.

CHAPTER III.

SECTION I.

Lady Campbell's Female Orphan Asylum at Fort St. George, founded 1787 A.D.

BUT the tasks they had to cope with were being rendered more difficult with the increase of population. We learn from the S.P.C.K. *Report* (1784) and the *History of the S.P.C.K.*[1] as quoted in *Penny*, that "a considerable number of children was being born annually in the British settlements in the East Indies, of fathers who were Europeans and mothers who were natives. That of this description there were born annually not less than 700 at Madras and on the coast of Coromandel." Due provision for these children made the foundation of

[1] By Allen and McClure (1898).

Chapter III. Sect. I.

Lady Campbell's Female Orphan Asylum.

other schools a necessity, and Lady Campbell, the wife of the Governor of Fort St. George, set to work about 1784 to raise money for the purpose.[1] The S.P.C.K. voted a sum of £50 to be paid as an annual stipend as soon as a school would be started. Money was freely given not only by the Company's servants but also by the Nawāb of Arcot, who expressed his wish to benefit the children of the soldiers by whose courage alone he still retained his position as a Nawāb. He purchased a large house with compound by the Mount Road (the house formerly belonging to Col. John Wood) at 8000 *pagodas* and presented it along with 1500 *pagodas* to Lady Campbell for the purpose of the school. The subscriptions from the local people amounted to 30,000 *pagodas*. In 1787 the Committee of Governors were in a position to commence their work. To start with, there were 62 girls in the

[1] *Penny*, Vol. I., pp. 507, 508.

Lady Campbell's Female Orphan Asylum.

school which obtained the name of *Female Orphan Asylum*. The Directors agreed to pay a subscription of Rs.5/- a month for each of the children and gave the standing order that their grant would continue at this rate until the number of children rose to 100. The appeal for this grant was made to them on the ground that similar liberality had been shown to the Orphan House at Calcutta, for which they had sanctioned an initial expenditure of Rs.89,687 and a monthly payment of Rs.5/- for each child.[1]

The Direction was to consist of the Governor, the members of the Council, and eight other gentlemen including two clergymen. The children were to be under governesses and nurses under the control of twelve Directresses. There were to be five classes of children, viz.:—

1. Female orphans of officers and soldiers.

[1] *Penny*, Vol. I., pp. 508-512.

Lady Campbell's Female Orphan Asylum.

2. Female children who had lost one parent.

3. Legitimate female children of soldiers and their European wives.

4. Legitimate female children of soldiers and their Indian wives.

5. Legitimate female children of European civilians of the settlement.[1]

The financial position of the Company was not good about this time, and as there were so many other pressing demands upon their funds, it is not a matter of surprise that there were arrears in payment of their contributions to the school from the very outset. However, they were paid off some time after.[2]

In appreciation of the excellent services of Lady Campbell in promoting the interests of the institution, she was made perpetual patroness of the Asylum, and the election of Governors was held on the anniversary of her birthday, the 20th March.[3]

[1] *Penny*, Vol. I., pp. 510–515; also *V.O.M.* Vol. III., pp. 354 ff.

[2] *Ibid.* [3] *Ibid.*

Chapter III. Sect. I.

Lady Campbell's Female Orphan Asylum.

Power was given to the Governors to apprentice the girls when necessary, and to the local Government authorities to inspect the school. The number of girls soon amounted to 108.[1]

The condition of the school in 1790 was satisfactory, as an extension of its buildings was made at a cost of 3000 *pagodas*. This year a necessity arose for making provision in the Asylum for 150 girls, because the Fort St. George Government was preparing for war with Ṭīpū Sulṭān, who was fanatically hostile to the English Company. He attacked the Rājā of Travancore, an ally of the Company; and the British soldiers, before going on active service, had to consider what would become of their children during their absence. They approached the Governors of the Asylum who in their turn approached the Government, representing that there was room in the school sufficient for 150 girls, and if the

[1] *Penny*, Vol. I., pp. 510–515.

Government grant was increased to Rs.750 a month (*i.e.* at the rate of Rs.5/- per mensem for each girl), provision could be made for the children of the soldiers departing for war. The Government, under the circumstances, could not but consent. In 1800, the Lady Directresses asked through their Secretary, the Rev. C. W. Gericke, for an extension of the Government bounty providing for 200 instead of 150 children on account of the increase of applications owing to the recent war. But the Government could not accommodate them owing to the bad state of its finances. There were several such subsequent appeals and as many refusals from the Directors.[1]

Section II.

Male Asylum—Bell's Educational System.

We shall now give an account of the *Male Asylum*, for the establishment of

[1] *Penny*, Vol. I., pp. 516-518.

which, steps were taken from June, 1787,[1] shortly after the Orphan Asylum for girls had been opened. The object of the new institution was to educate and maintain the orphan boys—mostly sons of soldiers in the service of the Company. The Madras Government sanctioned a monthly allowance of Rs.500/- at the rate of Rs.5/- a month for each boy in the school—the rate being similar to that for each girl in the Female Orphan Asylum. The St. Mary's Charity School for both boys and girls was left to pursue its own course, and the suggestion that it should be remodelled to meet the new emergencies found little support. A committee was formed of fifteen persons to consider the plan of the school and to arrange all the preliminaries. They asked

[1] "The Asylum was opened on the 1st June, 1787, and 21 children were admitted in that month, and 36 more in July. In the following February the total number stood at 62."—*V.O.M.* Vol. III., p. 352, quoting *Public Consultations*, Vol. 148, 4th March, 1788.

the Government to grant them the Egmore redoubt and about six acres of land around it, in addition to the aforesaid monthly allowance. Dr. Bell, the Presidency Chaplain, was the ex-officio Director of the school and its Superintendent.[1] A permanent council was formed consisting of Governor, members of the Council, Commander-in-Chief, two Chaplains and two Churchwardens of St. Mary's to act as Managers and Directors. There were also appointed twelve Sub-directors.

Dr. Bell, on his appointment, had a sub-committee formed to draw up the rules of the school. He abolished the distinction between the directors and sub-directors and also between the children of officers and others, and recommended a committee of three to represent the directors as a visiting and managing committee. They made an appeal to the public for help, decreed that the

[1] *Penny*, Vol. I., pp. 522-527.

education in the school was to be elementary,—confined to the three R's, and prescribed the boys' dress,—shirt, trousers and a coat for occasional use, and also fixed the master's pay at 20 *pagodas* for one, and 15 for another.[1]

As the result of the appeal, all ranks below Field-officers gave two days' pay to the school fund, while Generals and Field-officers paid more. Col. Floyd of the 19th Dragoons sent the pay of a suspended officer, while Col. Brathwaite and others the regimental fines for drunkenness. The Military Board remitted the unclaimed prize-money of former years, which amounted to 2270 *pagodas.*[2] After the Mysore war, more unclaimed prize-money was contributed, amounting to 14,000 *pagodas.* The school within a short time after its foundation was put on a secure financial footing, and its number of boys increased from 100 to 150 in 1790, and to 200 in 1792.

1 *Penny*, Vol. I., pp. 526–528. 2 *Ibid.*

Chapter III. Sect. II.

Male Asylum: Bell System of Education.

(a) *Bell System of Education—An Adaptation of the Indian Method.*

The method of education followed in this school was a new one. Dr. Bell had for a long time watched the system pursued in the village schools in Southern India, and the system which he prescribed for the school in his charge was a variation of this indigenous method. This method is known in England as the *Bell System*, which Dr. Bell has explained in his book entitled *An Experiment in Education.* The system is also called the *Madras System*, or the *Pupil-Teacher System.* It consisted in the elder or more advanced students teaching the younger. Each class of boys had an equal number of teachers and pupils. The teachers promoted to the next higher class became the taught, and at the next promotion became teachers of the new-comers. By this arrangement the master could do without assistants, an usher alone being needed. The system is no doubt excellent so far as elementary education is concerned.[1]

(b) *Cordiner's Account.*

James Cordiner, the successor of Bell, was full of admiration for this system. He says in his *Voyage to India*, "From the perpetual agency of this system, no idlers can exist. On entering the school, you can discover no individual unemployed, nobody looking vacantly round him, the whole is a picture of the most animated industry and resembles the various machinery of a cloth or thread manufactory completely executing their different offices and all set in motion by one active engine. It (the system) creates general activity and attention; it gives, as it were, to the master the hundred hands of Briareus, the hundred eyes of

[1] *Penny*, Vol. I., pp. 527–529; also Lawson's *Memories of Madras*, pp. 205–227.

Chapter III. Sect. II.

Male Asylum: Cordiner's Account.

Argus, and the wings of Mercury."[1] Cordiner records that on the eighteenth of June, 1798, he took charge of the school. The number of students therein was 280, the greater part of whom consisted of orphans, being sons of non-commissioned officers and private soldiers principally by Indian women, and the rest the children of officers, for each of whom a fee of 3 *pagodas* a month had to be paid.[2] "The same apartment," says he, "formed their schoolroom, their banqueting hall and their bedchamber; they ate their victuals at the same table at which they learned their tasks; the brick floor, the tables and the benches became their beds. Straw-mats indeed were spread upon the floor for the children to lie upon, but they never undressed. They had no bedclothes, and many of them preferred lying on the bare tables and benches which afforded them a situation a little elevated, pure air and

[1] Cordiner's *Voyage to India*, p. 87.

[2] *Ibid.*, pp. 81 ff.

greater coolness. Their dress was of pure white calico and very simple, consisting in general only of a shirt and trousers which they shifted four times a week. On Sundays and holidays when they went abroad, they were allowed the addition of sleeved waistcoats and leather caps. On similar occasions, some of the higher ranks of teachers were indulged with shoes; but no stockings were ever worn. Their principal food was rice with a little seasoning, and every meal was nearly the same. As a luxury on Sundays, they had mutton broth and a morsel of bread. . . . The tuition of the school was entirely conducted by the boys themselves. At least I was the only grown person among them in the character of a teacher. The school was divided into classes, the boys were paired off into tutors and pupils. The former were those of greater abilities or superior attainments. They assisted the latter in learning their lessons, and sitting continually by their side secured their

Chapter III. Sect. II.

Male Asylum: Cordiner's Account.

unremitting attention. . . . Every class had a teacher and an assistant who continually inspected the tutors and pupils, kept them busy, and heard them say their lessons as soon as prepared, which was generally once every half-hour. The teachers were from 7 to 14 years of age. The lessons were short, easy, and frequent, and every lesson was learned perfectly, before the scholars were allowed to proceed to another."[1] The way in which discipline was kept in the school is a novel one. A register of offences was kept by every boy in every class: a register of offences was also kept for the use of the whole school and the offences were tried weekly by a jury of their peers. This book was open to every inmate of the school who could note down in it any complaint or any trespass by teachers or pupils.[2]

[1] Cordiner's *Voyage to India*, p. 84.

[2] *Ibid.*

(c) *Cordiner's Account of Teaching the Alphabet.*

Cordiner describes a peculiar method of teaching the alphabet to the boys. A small quantity of dry sand was spread upon a table or a bench. The little tutor first traced a letter in the sand and the pupil followed his example.[1]

[1] Cordiner, p. 87. Cordiner remarks that this method of teaching the alphabet was universally practised in all the indigenous schools in India. Fryer, in his *New Account of East India and Persia*, records that the pedagogues used to teach children the alphabet with their fingers on the dust. After learning the alphabet, they used to write on a plastered board which was wiped out with cotton when full. Paper was given them last. Frederic Shoberl, in his *Hindustan in Miniature* (Vol. IV., pp. 210 ff.), also says that the boys in Malabar schools wrote the figures or letters with their fingers in the sand while repeating them with a loud voice. He also speaks of the practice of writing on small wooden tables covered with fine sand. The more advanced students wrote with styles on *ollas* or dried palm leaves. Writing on palm leaves with styles is an old practice that

Male Asylum: Cordiner's Account.

(d) *Cordiner's Account of Students' Daily Routine, etc.*

The same gentleman also gives us interesting details regarding the daily life of the students in the educational establishment. The children had to get up at about 5.30 a.m., wash and comb themselves by the side of a capacious tank and attend morning prayers at 7 o'clock. Then they took their breakfast, and at 8 attended school where they remained up to 12. They then dined at 1 p.m. and had to go to school again at 2, where they studied up to 5 in the afternoon, after which they walked attended by one of the masters. They supped at 6, attended

prevailed in Southern India. 'Abdur Razzaq also observed this mode of writing when he visited India in the fifteenth century (R. H. Major's *India in the Fifteenth Century*, p. 25). Alexander Hamilton also saw this practice in the first quarter of the eighteenth century (Pinkerton's *Collection of Voyages*, Vol. VIII., p. 410).

Chapter III. Sect. II.

Male Asylum: Cordiner's Account.

evening prayer at 7 and retired to rest at 8.[1]

They were taught reading, writing, arithmetic, book-keeping, geometry and navigation. They were likewise taught the principles of Christianity.[2]

The boys were admitted into the school at the age of 4 years, and at 14 were apprenticed to artificers, surveyors, clerks and sailors, or otherwise employed.[3] Three invalid soldiers acted as attendants in the school under the name of masters, and as guardians to the students when they walked abroad. Each of them had charge of a schoolroom and superintended the general economy of the school without having anything to do with the work of teaching.

1 Cordiner's *Voyage to India*, p. 84.

2 *Ibid.*

3 *Ibid.*

(e) *Finances.*

In view of the success of this school and its record of efficient work, the Madras Government recommended it to the directors for an increase of grant. The directors refused. The recommendation was repeated twice, but to no purpose. These refusals compelled the European residents in Madras, both official and non-official, to devise other means by which money could be raised for the school. In 1795 there were in it 250 sons of soldiers, the expenses for each being Rs.10 a month. The Company in paying Rs.5 a month for each boy may be taken as paying the entire cost of 50 boys; so that the remaining 200 had to be otherwise provided for. It must be said to the credit of all concerned that no suggestion was made of sending away a certain number of boys to shift for themselves in spite of the shortness of funds. The people of the place, on the other hand, raised money by the short

Chapter III. Sect. II.

Male Asylum: Finances.

cut to wealth often resorted to in the Company's settlements, viz. by lottery. The scheme for the lottery was matured by the representatives of nine of the principal mercantile firms. The lottery was advertised, from the profits of which permission was obtained from Government to appropriate 2000 *pagodas* for the benefit of the Asylum.[1]

In sanctioning the lottery in the cause of charity, the Madras Government hesitated for want of a precedent to follow. They knew of lotteries only in connexion with schemes of colonization, town-improvements, harbour-making and national profit. This technical difficulty was, however, got over by including in the scheme an item for repairing the Madras roads along with the obligation of assisting the Male Asylum.[2]

Thus the "Road and Asylum Lottery" was launched and turned out a great

[1] *Penny*, Vol. I., pp. 529, 530.

[2] *Ibid.*, p. 531.

Chapter III. Sect. II.

Male Asylum: Finances.

success. Subscriptions were paid by all communities, Europeans, Armenians, Hindus and Musalmāns. It answered its purpose so well that when the Madras Government prohibited lotteries in general on account of the scandals connected therewith, the Asylum lottery was excepted on the ground of its usefulness.[1]

The buildings, in which the boys were lodged and educated, consisted of three large open sheds with roofs of bamboo and tiles supported on wooden pillars. The Egmore redoubt was 100 feet square.

The buildings inside were pulled down on the north, south, and east sides, and on the west, a substantial house was built for the superintendent, the west wall being used for this building.[2]

The school, after the utilization of the lottery system, had no more to complain of want of funds. Between 1795 and 1805, 14 lacs of *pagodas* were raised.[3]

[1] *Penny*, Vol. I., pp. 530, 531.

[2] *Ibid.*, p. 529. [3] *Ibid.*, p. 531.

(f) *Dr. Bell's Achievements.*

The education in the Asylum, though *primâ facie* elementary, went further than reading, writing, and arithmetic in respect of meritorious boys. This was no doubt mainly due to the enthusiasm of Dr. Bell. He even gave lectures to the boys on natural philosophy and explained to them the use of scientific machines. To Captain Read is due the credit of educating the boys for the Revenue Department as intermediaries between the rulers and the ruled.[1] The reputation of the boys of the Asylum extended even to Ceylon, whence, in 1798, its Governor wrote to the Governor of Fort St. George for two boys of the Male Asylum to act as ushers in a school he was about to establish. They were offered 50 and 40 *pagodas* per month.[2]

[1] Southey's *Life of Bell*, Vol. I., as quoted in *Penny*, Vol. I., p. 532.

[2] *Penny*, Vol. I., pp. 531–533.

Male Asylum: Dr. Bell's Achievements.

Dr. Bell had to retire from office owing to ill-health in 1796. The Asylum lost by his retirement an enthusiastic patron who never showed any sign of abatement in his zeal for the promotion of its interests. It was this educationist who established and endowed a Bell lecturership at Edinburgh in connexion with the Theological Institution of the Episcopal Church of Scotland, and paid £120,000 to found a college at St. Andrew's where he was born and brought up. A portion of the inscription on the tablet that was placed in his honour in Westminster Abbey is as follows :—

" Andrew Bell, D.D., LL.D.,
Prebendary of this collegiate Church,
The eminent founder of the Madras system of education,
Who discovered and reduced to successful practice
The plan of mutual instruction,
Founded upon the multiplication of power and division of labour
In the moral and intellectual world
Which has been adopted within the British Empire

As the national system of education
Of the children of the poor,
etc., etc., etc."[1]

(g) *Dr. Bell's Successors.*

Bell was requested to choose his successor, and his choice fell on Mr. Cordiner, whom the Directors of the charity[2] undertook to pay £200 a year and an additional £120 for outfit. Cordiner, however, remained at the school only 11 months, and was succeeded by R. H. Kerr who continued till 1808.[3] He appointed Mr. Loveless, a London missionary, as a schoolmaster under him.[4] "Kerr laboured hard among the growing Eurasian population of the place, hunting up the children, bringing them in batches to be baptized, and seeing that those who were old enough to attend school were sent."[5]

1 *Penny*, Vol. I., pp. 680–681.

2 *Ibid.*, pp. 531–533.

3 *Ibid.*, p. 533.

4 *Ibid.*, p. 453.

5 Mrs. F. Penny's *Hist. of Fort St. George*, p. 181.

Chapter III. Sect. II.

Male Asylum: Dr. Bell's Successors.

Amongst his many good works may be mentioned the superintendence of the Male Asylum, and the introduction of the following change in the arrangement of the institution. It was a practice in the institution to apprentice the boys in some trade as a means of their future provision. Kerr was not satisfied with the results, and wanted to add an industrial department to the school. Though the Government gave him no encouragement in the matter, he employed his own capital for setting up a printing press in the school premises. It became not only a means of training to the boys but also a source of income to the school. In 1799 Kerr could present to the institution a sum of 1000 *pagodas* out of its profits. It was this press that afterwards became known as the Lawrence Asylum Printing Press used for printing Government papers.[1]

We cannot trace the history of the

[1] Mrs. F. Penny's *Hist. of Fort St. George*, p. 181.

Male Asylum further, as we cannot go beyond the eighteenth century. We have gone into some details regarding the Female Orphan Asylum and the Male Asylum with a view to give some idea not only of the rules and practices that prevailed at the time, which no doubt would be interesting to one who looks at them from the standpoint of modern days, but also the changes and developments they underwent by the force of circumstances.

SECTION III.

History of Educational Activity mainly outside Fort St. George.

(a) *Sullivan and Others.*

Let us now watch Schwartz, the S.P.C.K. missionary, pursuing his apostolic object by various methods, some of which were educational. Mr. John Sullivan, the representative of the Fort St. George Government at the Court of the Rājā of

Tanjore, came under the influence of Schwartz, and applied himself to the promotion of education. He introduced a change in the method of education hitherto followed. Boyle, Fell, and Prideaux advocated a century ago that teaching should be carried on in the vernacular; the clauses of the Charter of 1698 also obliged the Company to stick to the vernacular medium. English for the English, Portuguese for the Portuguese, and Tamil for the Tamils. Sullivan was for the establishment of English schools for all, as this would help not only the Company and the people to understand each other but would also facilitate dealings of all kinds between them. Schwartz entirely approved his plan, as it would help the pupils better to enter into the doctrines of the Gospel.[1] This scheme was placed for approval before the Governor Lord Macartney and the Nawab of Arcot from whom it was necessary to get permission and

1 *Penny*, Vol. I., pp. 518, 519.

Chapter III. Sect. III

History of Educational Activity mainly outside Fort St. George.

financial help before a beginning could be made. The Rājā of Tanjore, the ruler of the Maravar country at Ramnad, and the Zamindar of Shivagunga, before whom the plan was also laid, were impressed with the advantages that would accrue therefrom, and promised 480, 300, and 300 *pagodas* a year respectively. *Three schools were established at Tanjore, Ramnad and Shivagunga in* 1785, the Directors, when appealed to, contributing 250 *pagodas* annually for the up-keep of each of the schools, expressing the hope that more extensive benefactions might be forthcoming from the Indian princes.

Mr. J. C. Kohlhoff, son of a missionary at Tranquebar, was appointed superintendent of Tanjore English school, Mr. William Wheatley of the Ramnad school, and the Rev. C. Pohle of Trichinopoly, of the Shivagunga school. The schools were meant for the higher classes only, and the Rājā of Ramnad sent his son to the

Ramnad school for instruction.[1] This institution, however, flourished only for a short time. The S.P.C.K. authorities wrote to the Directors asking them to appoint committees at the two Presidencies of Madras and Bengal for superintending the schools that existed or might be established there for teaching English, and to take the financial management out of the hands of the missionaries. The Directors took no such steps. The Ramnad and Shivagunga schools had to pass, shortly after their establishment, through a series of misfortune. The Indian rulers were unable any longer to continue their grants-in-aid. The country in which they were situated was restored to the Nawab who resumed the system of oppression. After 1790, the two schools, it seems, ceased to exist. The same year, however, Schwartz opened another school at Combaconum with the consent and assistance of the Rājā of the place. This institution, together with that

[1] *Penny*, Vol. I., pp. 519, 520.

at Tanjore, was permanently endowed, while the other two schools that came to an end had not been similarly provided for.

Although these schools were under the direct management of the missionaries, Christianity was not expressly taught therein; nor were any deceitful methods used to instil Christian doctrines into the pupils' minds. It was, however, Schwartz's hope that the schools would have some indirect effect upon the students.

(b) *Educational Activity in Ceylon.*

A few other educational institutions besides those already mentioned were also founded. We learn from Dr. Prideaux's Report that before 1695 a college had been established by the Dutch in Ceylon chiefly for the instruction of the converts of the place.[1] Besides this, there were other educational institutions in the island.

[1] *Penny*, Vol. I., p. 120.

Cordiner, whom we have noticed before, was invited to the place by the Governor, the Hon. Frederick North, to act as the military chaplain of Colombo.[1] On the 21st of September, 1799, the Governor directed the formation of three schools at Colombo, one for the children of the higher classes of the Singalese, another for those of Malabars, and the third for those of Europeans. Cordiner was the principal of the schools. The course of study was to be concluded in six years, and to consist of reading and writing the Singalese language both modern and ancient, English, Malabar, and Portuguese, as well as the principles of religion according to the Church of England, arithmetic, agriculture, and ethics, together with a summary knowledge of the principles of the civil law of the place. The three schools which were established immediately, continued to flourish, especially the Singalese and Malabar schools

[1] *Penny*, Vol. I., p. 687.

under the charge of Mr. Armour. A proposal was made for the establishment of a higher school for those students who gave proofs of their talents in the three lower schools; but owing to opposition from the authorities the proposal was not carried out.[1]

There was another school in Ceylon at Cotta, in the Rygamcorte, which Cordiner visited on the 29th of November, 1799. There were in it altogether 129 boys and 32 girls. Of the boys, 20 could read and write, 35 could write in sand, and 74 were learning the letters.

The girls were not allowed to read or write, but were taught to repeat prayers, Catechism and the Creed, which they must be able to explain before they could obtain permission to marry.[2] Regarding Fort St. George, Cordiner records that besides the other institutions already noticed, there was a public school in the Black

[1] Cordiner's *Voyage to India*, pp. 193, 196.
[2] *Ibid.*, p. 218.

Chapter III. Sect. III.

History of Educational Activity mainly outside Fort St. George.

Town kept by an Englishman to which Christian students were admitted on payment of established fees.

In 1716 it appears that the S.P.C.K. missionaries founded charity schools outside Fort St. George.[1] In Trincombar and other neighbouring places there were a few charity schools.[2]

(c) *Grundler, an Educationist.*

In 1715–16 Mr. J. E. Grundler, a companion-helper of Ziegenbalg, reported to Mr. H. Newman, secretary to the S.P.C.K., that he had obtained permission from the English Governor to start a charity school either at Madras or Devanapatnam (Fort St. David). Schemes, however, for the schools were submitted to the Governors of both Fort St. George and Fort St. David and put in operation in both these places. The scheme

[1] *Penny*, Vol. I., p. 187.
[2] *Ibid.*

sent to the Governor of Fort St. George was as follows[1] :—

"1. *Whereas the slaves belonging to the English inhabitants of this place have a great many children who have no manner of care taken of them, but are kept entirely ignorant of the Christian religion, it is humbly proposed that a Charity School be erected wherein such poor children shall be taught to read and write the Portuguese language (which is the only one they understand), and be fully instructed and trained upon practical knowledge of religion and the true doctrines of the Gospel.*

"2. *There being some reason to hope that the knowledge of Christianity may also be propagated among the natives of this country, it is likewise proposed that a Malabar (*i.e. *Tamil) Charity School be erected in some convenient place in the Black Town, for instructing poor children in the principles of religion, and to teach them to read, write and cast accounts, after the way and manner used among the Malabars* (i.e. *the Tamils*).

"3. *That these two schools be allowed the protection and patronage of the Honourable Governor and Council, without whose consent and approbation, nothing of moment relating to the said schools shall be transacted.*

---

[1] *Penny*, Vol. I., pp. 190 ff.

An S.P.G. Mission School attached to the Tower of Christ Church, Old Town, Cuddalore, Madras. [From Rev. Frank Penny's *Church in Madras*, vol. i. (*Smith Elder & Co.*).]

"4. *That the immediate care and directions of the said two schools shall be committed to two or more Trustees to be appointed by the Honourable Governor for the time being.*

"5. *That leave be given to such Trustees to build or buy two school-houses, one for the Portuguese school within the English town, and another for the Malabar school in the Black Town.*

"6. *That what money, gifts or legacies shall be given by charitable persons for the support of the said two schools or either of them shall duly be registered by the Trustees in a book to be kept for that purpose.*

"7. *That the Trustees shall have power to make what particular orders and regulations shall be found necessary for the better management of the said two schools, provided that the said regulations shall be approved of by the Honourable Governor and Council.*" [1]

The scheme submitted to the Deputy Governor and Council of Fort St. David was similar to the above. In 1717 the Governor reported to the Directors that in the school at Cuddalore (a town outside Fort St. David) one master taught Tamil and another Portuguese,

[1] *Penny*, Vol. I., pp. 190–192.

Chapter III. Sect. III.

History of Educational Activity mainly outside Fort St. George.

and wrote in addition: "We have at Mr. Grundler's coming since to Madras, permitted him to erect a Portuguese school in the White town and a Malabar school in the Black."[1]

The arrangements for the management of the school were so similar to those for St. Mary's Charity School that we cannot help thinking that Mr. Stevenson must have consulted Grundler while he was drawing up the scheme for the Charity School.

(d) *Educationists other than Grundler.*

The Missionary schools had to meet with a bad time soon afterwards owing to the death of Ziegenbalg in 1719 and of Grundler in 1720. The return of Stevenson to England and the apathy of Charles Long, the Chaplain of Fort St. George, also contributed to aggravate the unfavourable situation. In 1726

[1] *Penny*, Vol. I., pp. 190, 191.

History of Educational Activity mainly outside Fort St. George.

Schultze, the successor of Grundler, took permission of the Fort St. George Governor to resuscitate the schools.[1]

In 1732 the S.P.C.K. obtained permission from the Directors for the building of two schools in Madras, one for boys and another for girls, rendered necessary for the instruction of the increasing number of converts.[2]

The Danish missionaries were very earnest in educational matters. They had founded schools at Tranquebar even before 1715. The Directors promised them assistance whenever they would extend their educational activities to the English settlements in the Madras Presidency.[3] From this time they worked with untiring energy which evoked an admiring report to Government in 1802 from Gericke, representing the good they had done among both

[1] *Penny*, Vol. I., p. 193.

[2] *Ibid.*, pp. 195, 196.

[3] *Ibid.*, p. 189.

Indians and Europeans by means of schools, poor relief, and dissemination of good literature.[1]

In 1742 Geisler and Kiernander founded charity schools for Eurasians as well as Indians in and near Fort St. David. It was in the school-chapel between the Garden House and the Fort that many Native-Christians sought refuge during the siege of the place by Count Lally and his force. But the refugees were inhumanly massacred and the chapel destroyed.[2] The general destruction by the French was very great; so that, when they were driven out of the place by a British force under Sir Eyre Coote, the missionaries had to commence their labours afresh without school or church to start with.[3] In 1772 Hutteman and Gericke revived the

[1] *Penny*, Vol. I., p. 253.

[2] *Ibid.*, p. 287; also *Calcutta Review* (1847), p. 132.

[3] *Penny*, Vol. I., p. 287.

English school at Cuddalore and carried it on along with the Portuguese and Tamil schools which they had already re-opened. Two old soldiers taught thirty European and British Eurasian children in the English school. The schools, however, met with a reverse of fortune by the death of Hutteman in 1781, after twenty-five years of useful service among all classes. He left small legacies to the schoolmasters who helped him in his educational work, viz. Sergeant George and Sergeant Connor. A part of his will was as follows: "If the Hon'ble Society will approve of combining the Cuddalore and Vepery Mission, for split ropes have no strength, and will order all the houses here, gardens and Devicottah acre, to be formed into one aggregate sum for the maintenance of a college to read publicly four hours a week on Divinity and Moral philosophy, I bequeathe to such an institution 500 *pagodas*. If not approved, the sum returns to my estate."[1] Soon after, however, Ḥaidar 'Alī and the French attacked Cuddalore. They did not remain long in possession, as they were turned out in 1782. The school buildings were not destroyed.[2]

In the village of *Vepery* there were *schools* for both Eurasians and Indians. A separate provision was also made in them for the support and education of Eurasian orphan girls. These institutions were conducted by the missionaries. Mr. Fabricius was the missionary in charge in 1765.[3] *Negapatam* contained a *charitable school* of which Domingo de Rozario was a schoolmaster. Gericke at his death left legacies both to the tutor and the charitable institution. The school obtained from the Company an allowance of 40 *pagodas* a month, which could not supply its needs, and the

[1] *Penny*, Vol. I., pp. 289, 290.
[2] *Ibid.*, pp. 290, 291.
[3] *Ibid.*, pp. 351, 352.

legacy was meant to augment this allowance. Gericke also made a similar provision for the schools at Vepery.[1]

At *Bombay* a school was opened in 1719 under the auspices of the Rev. Mr. Richard Cobbe. He preached a sermon on the 8th September of that year, after which a sum was collected. The institution started with the fund was named the *Charity School*, and was the origin of what were later on known as the Education Society Schools at Byculla. The school was meant for the education of Protestant children and located within the Fort, where it continued till 1825, when it was removed by the order of Government to the present buildings at Byculla constructed at the cost of Rs.175,000/-. Forbes in his *Oriental Memoirs* refers to the institution : "There was also a Charity School for boys and a fund for the poor belonging to the

[1] *Penny*, Vol. I., p. 267 ; also Taylor's *Memoir*, Appendix, p. xxx.

Chapter III. Sect. III.

History of Educational Activity mainly outside Fort St. George.

'Church of England.' The Rev. Mr. Cobbe himself would most probably have brought his benevolent scheme to completion, if, as a writer of the *Bombay Quarterly Review* says, untoward circumstances had not checked him in his useful career and driven him to leave India in disgust." The untoward circumstances were that he was removed from the place for sedition of which Government suspected him.[1]

It appears that shortly after 1580, a *Jesuits' College* was established in Chaul, which was attended by more than 300 alumni. Latin, logic, theology, rudiments of Portuguese grammar, and music were taught here.[2]

There were *other colleges also in the Bombay Presidency at this early period.* Thomas Stevens, who landed in Goa in 1579, was "engaged in the rectorship of

[1] Da Cunha's *The Origin of Bombay*, p. 364.

[2] Da Cunha's *History of Chaul and Bassein*, p. 96.

Chapter III. Sect. III.

History of Educational Activity mainly outside Fort St. George.

a Jesuit College at Margao first and at Rachol afterwards in the *Salsette of Goa.*"[1]

There was also a *Jesuit College* called the *College of St. Anne* at Bandora (in Salsette) which was constructed in 1620. *Another College* was at Monpacer, over the door of which "is an inscription in Portuguese with the arms of Portugal above it, purporting that the erection was made in 1623 (1643?) by order of Infant Dom John III. of Portugal (King Dom Joao IV.?)."[2]

Two colleges, one of the Jesuits and the other of the Franciscans, were established at Bassein. It is difficult to say when they were founded, but one of them seems to have existed in 1575, and

[1] *Institute Vasco da Gama,* Vol. II., pp. 245, 263, 283 *et seqq.*; and *Times of India Handbook of Hindustan,* p. 116, as quoted in Da Cunha's *History of Chaul and Bassein,* p. 188; and Da Cunha's notes thereon.

[2] Da Cunha's. *History of Chaul and Bassein,* pp. 197, 199, 195.

Chapter III. Sect. III.

History of Educational Activity mainly outside Fort St. George.

both of them were visited by Fryer in the middle of the seventeenth century.[1]

In 1790 there also existed at Bombay a "Portuguese Eurasian School" of which Mr. Kerr, already mentioned in another connexion, was a superintendent for two years. Kerr, it should be noticed in passing, was the founder of a school in *Black Town* in Madras. The institution was started in 1792 with assistance from Mr. Basil Cochrane.[2]

In 1773 Fabricius established a school at Vellore for the European children of the place. The local officers helped him much in this undertaking. From 1792 onwards, for a few years, Mr. William Harcourt Torriano also took much care for the education of native Christians.[3]

I shall conclude my account of schools

[1] Da Cunha's *History of Chaul and Bassein*, pp. 196, 228; and also *Ibid.*, p. 230, quoting Churchill's *Voyages*, Vol. IV., p. 192.

[2] *Penny*, Vol. I., p. 682.

[3] *Ibid.*, p. 622.

established by Europeans with the observations of Fra Paolino da San Bartolomeo, who came to Pondichery in 1776 and remained there for thirteen years. At Virapatnam (*i.e.* Strong City), about six miles to the south-west of Pondichery, there was a seminary which he visited. It was founded by M. Mathon, a missionary who presided over it as a Rector. As Paolino gives minute details about the inner life of the school, it is better to allow him to speak in his own language.

The building was situated in a palm-garden and "resembled a convent, but was much better divided; and so contrived that these Oriental seminarists did not find the least impediment either in their study, their bodily exercise or their other labours. Between three side-apartments where the three tutors lodged, was a large hall on the ground-floor in which were constructed two rows of small chambers all adjoining. They were separated from each other by thin

Chapter III. Sect. III.

History of Educational Activity mainly outside Fort St. George.

wooden partitions of only three or four palms in height; so that each of the students had an apartment to himself and all of them could be observed by their teacher. The teacher sat at a desk where he read his lessons; and while employed in teaching, he could with one view see everything that was doing in the different apartments. The pupils not only studied in these apartments but also slept in them. A table on which lay a mattress supplied the place of a bed; and both above and beneath it another table was suspended which could be lowered or raised up at pleasure. If any of these young people wished to write, he had no occasion to leave his chamber, as he had nothing to do but to sit down at the foot of his bed; and when he wished to go out, he had only to remove his table and fold it up. On the other table above the bed were books, paper, pens and ink, his long seminary dress, and several small articles necessary for preserving cleanliness. The doors of the hall, which were exactly opposite to each other, stood always open to afford a free passage to fresh air; but no one could go out unperceived by the tutor, who in his apartment was continually observing everything that passed. The rectory was situated in another part of the building; and it was customary to read in it during meals. The shops of the tailor, shoemaker and carpenter, together with the printing office and ovens for baking bread, were without, and all occupied by seminarists; for each of them was obliged to learn a trade. They all went bare-footed; and one of their employments was to water and look after the young palm-trees which were planted in the garden. Their time was so divided, that they studied daily four hours; devoted one hour to manual labour; and spent the remaining part in prayer, singing and meditation. On two days in the week they conversed

Chapter III. Sect. III.

History of Educational Activity mainly outside Fort St. George.

in their mother-tongue, but on other days they were obliged always to speak Latin. M. Mathon showed me a bull of his present Holiness Pope Pius VI. issued in favour of this seminary and in which he bestowed great praises upon it. This institution was destined merely for young persons from China, Cochin China, Tunquin and Siam."[1]

Paolino does not give us any details as to other schools established in Southern India by the Europeans, but records that over and above other functions, a Malayala (Malabar) missionary was obliged to instruct children.[2]

[1] Fra Paolino da San Bartolomeo's *Voyage to the East Indies*, pp. 18–21. A letter of Hieronymus (1570) says that Cochin had two grammar schools containing 260 pupils. In connexion with the early educational efforts, the names of Robert de Nobili, John de Britto, Beschi, Arnauld and Calmette should be noted. They laboured in Madura, Trichinopoly, etc. (See Hunter's *Imp. Gaz.*, 2nd ed., Vol. VI., and *Indian Empire.*)

[2] *Paolino*, p. 201.

CHAPTER IV.

(a) *Early European Libraries in Southern India.*

FORT ST. GEORGE as well as Fort St. David possessed Government libraries. The one at Fort St. George did not come into existence till 1661, when Mr. Whitefield, the chaplain, set afoot a movement for the establishment of a library. Whitefield's spiritual charge was not a heavy one. He was alone at the Fort and had a good deal of time on his hands, which made him sigh for books. He brought it to the notice of the local merchants and Government authorities that the Fort badly needed a library. The merchants appear to have raised a sum of money for the purpose, which they invested in a bale of calico. They

Chapter IV.

Early European Libraries in Southern India.

despatched this bale home in the ships of January, 1661–62, to be sold in London by the Governor of the Company and the sale-proceeds to be utilized in the purchase of the books named in a list. The bale of calico was sold for £85 sterling, out of which 23½ pieces of gold were returned to Whitefield, the remainder being used for the books. The Directors took a hint from this, and purchased books, a year later, to the value of £20 which they directed to be kept in the Fort for the succeeding Ministers. These presentations were the origin of the Company's library at the Fort.[1]

The Directors used to send at intervals books to be put in the libraries of the Company. About 1669, they voted £5 for the purchase of certain books required for the Minister, Mr. Thomas Bill, which were to be added to the Fort St. George library. It seems that with the sum, the works of *Cornelius à Lapide* were

[1] *Penny*, Vol. I., pp. 38, 39.

purchased.[1] Shortly after, the Directors sanctioned £30 for books for the same library.[2] In 1675 Mr. Portman, the new chaplain, asked for a further addition of books to the library, which the authorities allowed, but wrote as follows to the Fort St. George Governor: "Herewith you have a catalogue of such books as were desired by Mr. Portman to be provided, which we send as an addition to our library; and in regard we find every chaplain we send as desirous of an addition; and that we have no perfect list here, we do require you to send us by the return of these ships a perfect catalogue of all our books both with you at Metchlepatam and the Bay."[3]

The library at Masulipatam existed even before 1671, in which year the books left by Mr. Hook, the chaplain, dying at the place, were added to the Masulipatam

[1] *Penny*, Vol. I., p. 53.
[2] *Ibid.*, p. 54.
[3] *Ibid.*, p. 60.

library.[1] In 1678 this library contained 73 books in all, which with very few exceptions were theological.[2]

In 1676 the Directors despatched a few sets of books presumably for the various factory libraries. They wrote, "There being two useful treatises lately extant, the one touching the existence of God, the other against Popery, we have thought it fit to send ten of the one and four of the other."[3]

In 1695, 300 Portuguese liturgies were sent out for distribution among the inhabitants of the English settlements. The Directors, however, made a mistake; for the sort of Portuguese which was their *lingua franca* was very different from the pure Portuguese in which the books were written. When they found out this mistake, they ordered the books to be kept in the Church library of Fort St. George and given in future only to those

[1] *Penny*, Vol. I., p. 52.
[2] *Ibid.*, p. 69. [3] *Ibid.*, p. 65.

Portuguese who understood them. The books, however, could be lent to borrowers from the library, a good list of whom was kept. On failure to return them when demanded back, the penalty was a fine of one *pagoda* each.[1]

Fort St. David, which is a later possession of the Company, was furnished with a library a few years after its acquirement. Mr. Laudon was the chaplain of the new Company at the Fort which he left in 1707. He had a collection of books which he did not take away. The Company, it seems, purchased these books, which became the nucleus of the Fort St. David Library.[2]

Fort St. George about this time began to accumulate a goodly number of books in its library. The traveller Lockyer, who visited the Fort in 1703, says that books of Divinity in the library were worth £438 6*s*. at the time.[3]

1 *Penny*, Vol. I., p. 113. 2 *Ibid.*, p. 126.
3 *Ibid.*, p. 132; see also *V.O.M.*, Vol. II., p. 83.

Chapter IV.

Early European Libraries in Southern India.

It was Lockyer's book that made the Directors pay more attention to this library, which had now developed by slow accretions of about sixty years into a decent collection. About 1714 they wrote to the officers at the Fort as follows: "We understand that the library in Fort St. George is worthy of our notice as consisting not only of a great number of books but of a great many that are choice and valuable, John Dolben, Esquire, and Master Richard Elliot and others having made a present of their books (which were considerable) to the library, besides other augmentations it hath lately received from the Society for Promoting Christian Knowledge. We therefore recommend the care of the library to our President and Ministers, etc. We order our Ministers to sort the said books into proper classes and to take a catalogue of them to be kept in the library, of which they shall deliver a copy to our President and send a copy home to us; and we desire our President to order two of our servants together with our Ministers to examine the books by the catalogue once a year, that is to say, some few days before the vestry is held, and make their report at the vestry. It would be proper also to put our Chop (stamp) on the said books, etc."[1] This order came at the right moment, for the library at Fort St. David by that time had lost many of its books through want of care, and it was not improbable that at Fort St. George books might have been similarly abstracted. In 1716 the catalogue was sent to the Directors, who were much dissatisfied with the manner in which it was made, and ordered for a better catalogue. This order was not timely carried out, for which the Directors wrote with some warmth to the Fort authorities. It was not until 1720 that

[1] *Penny,* Vol. I., pp. 146–151; also *V.O.M.*, Vol. II., p. 150.

the library was arranged and the catalogue drawn up by the new chaplain, Mr. Thomas Wendey, for which he was promptly rewarded by the Governor and Council with a palanquin allowance.[1]

The Directors, at the request of the local authorities in the English settlements, used to send books either for addition to the libraries or for free distribution among schoolboys and others desirous of reading them. Sometimes they allowed the transmission of books in their ships free of passage—a concession which helped much the missionaries in the importation of books into this country. About 1714 they allowed Ziegenbalg, for instance, to bring books with him freight-free,[2] and within a year or two repeated the same favour.[3] It also appears from a few letters bearing dates from 1726 to 1741 that during the interval the Directors showed the same

[1] *Penny*, Vol. I., pp. 146–151.

[2] *Ibid.*, p. 187. [3] *Ibid.* p. 190.

spirit of kindliness and co-operation to the S.P.C.K. missionaries.[1] But at times, complaints were made of the apathy of the Directors in this matter. In 1785 the chaplains complained that no attention had been paid to their indent for religious as well as other books for four years. In 1787 an application for books was again made to the Directors on the ground that the last supply had long since been distributed among the Company's soldiers at Vellore, Vizagapatam, and Fort St. George, and that there was now a great demand for them in Wallajabad, Arcot, etc.[2] St. Mary's parish did not receive supplies of books for seven years until 1791, when the Directors sent it a supply. The chaplains of the parish were again disappointed in this matter for two years, for which they were unable to comply with the many applications that were made to

[1] *Penny*, Vol. I., pp. 198, 199.
[2] *Ibid.*, p. 373.

Chapter IV.

Early European Libraries in Southern India.

them from every quarter. Unfortunately, however, the *Winterton* that carried the books for them, after the long interval, was lost, and a fresh supply was not received until 1794. This time, however, the home authorities made amends by despatching twice the usual number of books. The chaplains had to write again six years after, and a supply was sent in the following year.[1]

It was no doubt financial pressure that obliged the Directors to be illiberal in this respect. As soon as it was removed by the defeat of Ṭīpū Sulṭān, their former liberality asserted itself. Since then, there were periods of strict economy and retrenchment, but none like that between 1782 and 1799.[2]

A complete record of the instalments of books sent by the Directors to the English settlements in India, before and in the eighteenth century, is difficult to

1 *Penny*, Vol. I., pp. 373, 374.
2 *Ibid.*

obtain; because such record is buried in heaps of old letters, reports and other documents which will have to be ransacked before such information can be procured. However, what has been stated above is sufficient to show that, taking all the circumstances into consideration, the Directors cannot be pronounced to have been illiberal in this direction.

(b) *Early European Libraries in Bengal.*

It appears that there existed already a library in Bengal in 1700, as it is stated that Benjamin Adams, the chaplain of the Bay, made an addition to it on his arrival in Calcutta on the 16th June of that year.[1] The S.P.C.K. sent out in 1709 a circulating library to Calcutta, the first of its kind in India.[2] In 1714

[1] Hyde's *Parish of Bengal*, p. 15.

[2] Long's *Handbook of Bengal Missions*, p. 6; Carey's *Good Old Days of Hon. John Company*, Vol. II., p. 34.

Chapter IV.

Early European Libraries in Bengal.

and 1715 the Governors of the S.P.C.K. sent parcels of books to Briercliffe, which were allowed by the Company to be carried free of charge in their ships.[1]

[1] Hyde's *Parochial Annals of Bengal*, p. 65.

Chapter V.

Caligraphy as a Means of Diffusion of Learning among Musalmāns.

CHAPTER V.

(a) *Caligraphy as a Means of Diffusion of Learning among Musalmāns.*

CLOSELY connected with the diffusion and promotion of education is the means by which copies of books can be multiplied cheaply and speedily. It was the practice with the Muhammadans to engage expert caligraphists for making copies. Many such experts were attached to the libraries of the Muhammadan rulers whose number varied in proportion to the amount of work required. Titles were conferred upon them according to the degrees of their skill in the art.[1]

[1] Such titles as Zarrīn-raqam (Golden writer), Shīrīn-raqam (Sweet writer), Raushan-raqam (Bright writer), Mushkīn-raqam (Perfumed writer) used to be conferred on the caligraphists.

(b) *Printing—its late adoption by Indians; an Account of its Introduction in India by Europeans.*

It is, however, strange that so long after the art of printing had been introduced into Southern India in the European settlements it came to be prevalent among the people of this country. This was perhaps due to the conservatism of the Indians; but Ovington, who visited India about 1689, gives perhaps the true reason why printing was not so readily adopted by them, in spite of its obvious advantages. Says he: "Neither have they (Indians) endeavoured to transcribe the art of printing; that would diminish the repute and livelihood of their scrivans who maintain numerous families by their pen. But they can imitate a little the English manner of binding books."[1] Fra Paolino

[1] Rev. J. Ovington's *A Voyage to Surat in 1689*, pp. 251, 252.

da San Bartolomeo gives us some information about the first introduction of printing in India which enables us to calculate the long time that elapsed before it received any recognition among the people of this country. "The art of printing in all probability never existed in India; and perhaps we should not be far wrong if we ascribed, in a great measure to this circumstance, the natural simplicity and the irreproachable manners of the inhabitants. They copy no other writings than such as are useful and good. The first book printed in this country was the *Doctrina Christiana* of Giovanni Gonsalvez, a lay brother of the order of the Jesuits, who, as far as I know, first cast Tamulic characters in the year 1577. After this appeared, in 1578, a book entitled *Flos Sanctorum*, which was followed by the *Tamulic Dictionary* of Father Antonio de Proenza printed in the year 1679 at Ambalacate on the coast of Malabar. From that period the

Chapter V.

Printing: its Introduction in India.

Danish missionaries at Tranquebar have printed many works, a catalogue of which may be found in *Alberti Fabricii Salutaris Lux Evangelii.*"[1] Da Cunha gives us, however, an account of the introduction of the art of printing in India which differs from Paolino's on some points. Da Cunha says that the art was introduced by the Portuguese missionaries as early as 1556, the first printer being Jao (Juan) de Bustamante. The first work issued from their press, according to him, was the *Catechismo de Doctrina* of St. Francis Xavier printed in 1557, five years after the author's death. But it appears from another source that the first book printed by Brother Juan was the *Theses* (or *Propositions to be Defended*), the next work being the *Catechismo.*[2] The second work

[1] Paolino's *A Voyage to the East Indies*, p. 395.

[2] *J. and P.* of A.S.B., Vol. IX. (1913), p. 155—*Imprentas de los Antiguos Jesuitas*, &c., by Gomes Rodeles.

published in the press according to Da Cunha, was the *Compendio Espiritual da Vida Christa,* by Dom Gaspar de Leao Pereira, the first Archbishop of Goa, printed by Hoao Quinquenio in 1561 and re-edited in Coimbra by Manuel de Araujo in 1600. The third was the *Colloquios,* by Garcia da Orta.[1]

Besides the one at Goa, there were four other printing presses set up by the Portuguese in Southern India. The first was at "Ambalacatta" (from *ambala-kadu*), which was a town of considerable importance about 1550. Here the Portuguese had built a church and a seminary and held the famous Synod of Diamper in 1599. It was at this time the centre of Portuguese missionary activities in Southern India and a place where Sanskrit, Tamil and Syriac languages were cultivated.[2] The three other printing

[1] Da Cunha's *The Origin of Bombay,* pp. 103, 104.

[2] *Ibid.*

Chapter V.

Printing: its Introduction in India.

presses were at Cochin, Angamale, and Panikkayal. We have already learnt from Paolino that Tamulic characters were first cast in 1577 by Gonsalvez and that the *Flos Sanctorum*, above referred to, was published at Panikkayal in 1578.[1] In 1579 a book on the Christian Doctrine was printed in the Malabar language.[2] Da Cunha adds that it was at Cochin that the types were cut and some important works in Tamil printed in the press.[3] It is noteworthy that Abul Faẓl does not make a single reference to printing or printed books while speaking of writing, either in his *Ā'īn* or in his *Letters*.

From this, it seems that printing did

1 *J. and P.* of A.S.B. (1913), p. 164.

2 *Ibid.*, p. 166.

3 Da Cunha's *The Origin of Bombay*, pp. 103, 104; *vide* also *Materials for the History of Oriental Studies amongst the Portuguese* by the same writer in *Atti Del IV. Congresso Internazionale degli Orientalisti*, Florence, 1880, pp. 185 ff.

not become popular at the time when Abul Faẓl wrote. Had it been so, it is not likely that he would have omitted to refer to it in his works.

(c) *First Printing in British India.*

The first printing press in British India was established at Madras by the S.P.C.K. in 1711 and an edition of the Tamil New Testament issued from it in 1714.[1] In Bengal a printing press was set up at Hughli in 1778 and Halhed's Bengali Grammar was printed in it. Sir Charles Wilkins prepared the types for this grammar and taught type-cutting to a blacksmith named Pañchānan.[2] This printing press is regarded by some as the first in Bengal, but that notion seems to be unfounded.[3] It is not my

[1] Long's *Handbook of Bengal Missions*, p. 5.

[2] Carey's *Good Old Days of Hon. John Company*, Vol. I., p. 299; also T. Singh in the *Calcutta Review*, Vols. VI. and XIII.

[3] That there were other printing presses in Bengal before the one at Hughli appears from

Chapter V.

First Printing in British India.

object to follow out the later history of the establishment of the printing presses in the different provinces of India, the first introduction of the art, which has been already treated, being its most interesting portion.

Mr. Carey's statement that the *India Gazette* was published in Calcutta before 1774 (Carey's *Good Old Days*, Vol. I., pp. 285).

BOOK II.

NORTHERN INDIA.

CHAPTER I.

CALCUTTA AND ITS VICINITY.

(a) *Bellamy's Charity School.*

WHILE the various European communities established schools and colleges in Southern India where they had settled, Bengal also, where they had commenced to trade and which was rising into importance as a place of European activities, received its due share of attention in respect of education; schools were started and the first educational institution was a charity school established in Calcutta by the English. It was opened, according to the Rev. J. Long, under the auspices of the S.P.C.K., in 1731;[1] but Mr. Hyde, on the authority of some letters written by the Chaplain Bellamy and "an

[1] Rev. J. Long's *Handbook of Bengal Missions*, pp. 5, 6.

Bellamy's Charity School.

eminent merchant" in January and February, 1731–32, inclines to the view that the school-house was completed that year and that the institution had already been in existence for some time.[1] The foundation of such a school had long been a cherished object of the S.P.C.K. and of the Rev. S. Briercliffe, the chaplain of Calcutta.[2] In 1709 Briercliffe had offered to superintend a school in Calcutta,[3] but his scheme, which met with many obstacles, was not brought into actual operation till 1720, when poor Tomlinson, the successor of Briercliffe, bequeathed to the school fund Rs.80/- and, shortly after, his widow Rs.40/- by their respective wills.[4] The school premises, built in 1731, was spacious enough for eight foundationers and forty day-scholars. It was due to the

[1] Hyde's *Parochial Annals of Bengal*, p. 86.

[2] *Ibid.*, p. 86.

[3] Long's *Handbook of Bengal Missions*, p. 5.

[4] Hyde's *Parochial Annals of Bengal*, p. 86, and his *Parish of Bengal*, p. 31.

Chapter I.

Bellamy's Charity School.

untiring energy of Bellamy, the chaplain, that the school about this time came to have an income, enough for the maintenance of the former and the tuition of all the scholars in the institution.[1] He roused the interest of the people in the school to which contributions were made by them liberally. "An eminent merchant," identified by tradition with Mr. Bourchier, then second of Council and afterwards Governor of Bombay (1750–1760), bore a large share of the cost of construction of the school-house.[2] The Mayor's Court, which tried suits in which Europeans were concerned, was founded by the Royal Charter in 1727, and to it were let out some apartments of the school-building for being used as its record-rooms at the rent of Rs.194–6–6 for every six months. The Mayor's Court, however, in course of time, was held in the hired apartments and the school was

[1] Hyde's *Parochial Annals*, p. 87.

[2] *Ibid.*, p. 87.

housed elsewhere, so that about 1753 the portion of the premises that was not used for the court was hired out for public purposes, *e.g.* balls, assemblies, etc., resulting in great advantage to the charity-stock. The building was, therefore, variously termed the "Court-House," the "Town House," or the "Town Hall."[1]

Bellamy made over the charge of the charity school to the Rev. Robert Mapletoft (*circa* 1750), who improved the school regulations and succeeded by his energy in increasing the charity-stock by fresh donations. He knew Portuguese and was allowed to reside for some time near the Court of the Nawāb of Murshidabad, in order that he might havė greater facilities in learning Persian.[2]

The foundationers of the charity school were habited almost in the same

[1] Hyde's *Parochial Annals*, p. 89.

[2] *Ibid.*, p. 103; and Hyde's *Parish of Bengal*, p. 52.

manner as their brethren in the schools in Southern India, of whom we have spoken before. They were dressed in blue coats and had to go about barefooted—a feature also noticeable in their successors in the Calcutta Free School with which the charity school was amalgamated in 1800.[1]

It seems that the first schoolmaster, unless the parish clerk had that charge, was a Franciscan Friar of Goa named Aquiere, who had been received into the Church of England by Bellamy about 1730.[2] He was paid Rs.30/- a month.[3]

(b) *Kiernander's School.*

The school met with a reverse of fortune in 1756, when Calcutta was attacked by the Muhammadans. After the recovery of the town, Colonel Clive,

Hyde's *Parochial Annals*, p. 89.

[2] *Ibid.*, p. 87; and Long's *Handbook*, p. 6 (Rev. J. Long does not express any doubt as to Aquiere's being the first schoolmaster).

[3] Hyde's *Parish of Bengal*, p. 39.

Chapter I.

Kier-nander's School.

who had witnessed the good results of Mr. Kiernander's missionary labours in the Madras Presidency, invited him to Calcutta. On the 1st of December next, after his arrival in Calcutta in 1758, he opened a school which by the middle of the next month came to have 48 scholars —Armenians 7, Portuguese 15, Bengalis 6, and Englishmen 20,—these last being the 20 boys maintained by the charity-stock.[1] The parish clerk continued to be the schoolmaster. Within a year, the number of pupils amounted to 174.[2] The building formerly used as the Collector's Office was made over to Kiernander by the Council for accommodating the charity school.[3]

Owing to the epidemic that raged in Calcutta in 1762, the children were withdrawn from the school by their guardians. But Mr. Kiernander's zeal remained

1 Hyde's *Parochial Annals*, p. 119, and Long's *Handbook*, p. 10.

2 *Ibid.*

3 *Ibid.*, p. 130.

unabated and the school flourished as formerly with the disappearance of the epidemic. In 1773 Kiernander's wife died and bequeathed her jewels with 6000 rupees, for the erection of some schoolrooms.

This lady appears to have been as generous as her worthy husband, who devoted about £12,000 to charitable purposes from his own pocket.[1]

Up to the end of 1787, no more than 20 boys were maintained in the school, but the increased income derived from its capital and cash, which by the time amounted to 2¼ lacs, enabled it to expand its useful work and make arrangements for the education of girls also. So in January, 1787, four destitute girls were elected, and owing to want of accommodation in the school-house, they were boarded out with a Mrs. Jane Jarvis at Rs.35/- a month for each, exclusive of clothing. It was afterwards proposed to

[1] Long's *Handbook*, pp. 11, 13, and 6.

maintain 20 girls, and about January 17, there were 32 boys in the institution, of whom 10 were probably day-scholars.[1]

From 1777 to 1784, the Rev. John Christman Diemer was the schoolmaster on a salary of 100 Arcot rupees per month. He had two ushers to assist him at Rs.150 a month each. The total expenses of the school amounted to more than Rs.900 per mensem.

In 1788 the parish clerk named William Aldwell was appointed a tutor in the school.[2] By the end of the year, Robert Hollier, another parish clerk, succeeded to the same post on Rs.100/- a month, with Thomas Kincey as his assistant, the whole establishment remaining under the supervision of the Senior Chaplain, Rev. William Johnson. Just before Johnson's resignation, the vestry decided to house the entire school, including boys and girls, in premises at

[1] Hyde's *Parochial Annals*, p. 198.

[2] *Ibid.*, p. 233.

Cossipore which was leased for two years at Rs.400/- a month, the landlord, Mr. Siderman, undertaking to convey the boys by water to and fro St. John's Church on Sunday mornings for divine service. On May 1, 1788, the boys were removed to this new abode, and on June 15, the girls also were taken there from the charge of Mrs. Jarvis. One Mrs. Clerke was elected as the mistress of the girls in place of Mrs. Jarvis, but she died before taking charge of the duties, and a Mrs. Tilsey succeeded her.[1] In 1789 Hollier was still the schoolmaster with Kincey as his assistant, whose wife Isabella, with two[2] other ladies, at Rs.16/- a month each, had charge of the girls.

(c) *Calcutta Free School: Kiernander's School Amalgamated.*

The affairs of the school went on satisfactorily for over a year, when it

[1] Hyde's *Parochial Annals*, p. 236.
[2] *Ibid.*, p. 230.

became apparent that this institution was unable to cope with the increasing need for charitable education of the destitute children. Accordingly, a public meeting was called on December 21, 1789, with the Governor-General in the chair, and it was resolved to found a society to be called the *Free School Society of Bengal*, the management being placed in the hands of the Governor-General as patron, the Select Vestry and six other gentlemen, the Churchwardens being perpetual treasurers of the funds. Four Honorary Governesses were also to be elected. The Free School had not commenced work when a proposal was made for uniting it with the charity school[1] which

[1] Hyde's *Parochial Annals*, p. 239. In Long's *Handbook* (p. 441) the Calcutta Free School is described as "the oldest charity school in Calcutta commenced about 1750. Besides the original subscriptions, the bulk of the funds of this school arose from the restitution-money, received for pulling down the English Church by the Moors at the capture of Calcutta in 1756. The interest of this property and on a

Chapter I. — Calcutta Free School.

was carried out on the 28th February, 1790, when the two years' lease of the Cossipore House expired and a large house belonging to Mr. Charles Weston was rented for the purpose.[1] In 1795 a garden house was purchased in Jān Bāzār for Rs.28,000, and in 1796 a school for girls was also erected.[2]

Two distinct establishments and two sets of accounts, however, continued to be kept for what was practically one

legacy of 6000/- or 7000/- rupees, left by Mr. Constantine, the rent of the old Court-house, formerly appropriated to the school and transferred to the Government for a perpetual payment of 800/- rupees per mensem, and the Church collections, maintained about 20 boys and enabled the vestry to bestow in addition some trifling charitable donations. In course of years, the old charity school became quite inadequate to the demand for education . . . and the Free School Society was established on the 21st of December, 1789." See also Carey's *Good Old Days of Hon. John Company*, Vol. I., pp. 404, 405.

1 Hyde's *Parochial Annals*, p. 239.

2 Carey's *Good Old Days of Hon. John Company*, Vol. II., p. 157.

school, and it was not till 1800 that they were consolidated into one.[1] On the 1st April, 1790, there were 17 boys and 12 girls on the Free School establishment, and by December, 1791, the numbers increased to 50 boys and 30 girls, and 21 day-scholars.[2] In 1800 there were 159 children in the amalgamated schools.[3]

(d) *Mushroom Schools.*

As the later history of this institution is beyond the scope of this work, we shall now speak of other schools established in Bengal during the period under review. It should, however, be remarked at the outset that about this time, along with the institutions that had a *bonâ fide* educational object in view, came also into existence many mushroom schools which were mere make-shifts for earning a living for their needy founders. It was schools

[1] Hyde's *Parochial Annals*, p. 243.
[2] *Ibid.*, p. 239. [3] *Ibid.*, p. 244.

of the latter type that have been humorously described by Mr. Carey: "Living upon a rupee a day, the old pensioners (*i.e.* invalid soldiers who had fought at Seringapatam or helped to drive the enemy from the plains of Plassey) smoked and walked, and smoked and slept their time away. One more learned, perchance, than the rest, opened a school, and while the modest widow taught but the elements of knowledge in the barracks of Fort William, the more ambitious pensioner proposed to take them higher up the hill of learning. 'Let us contemplate him seated in an old fashioned chair with his legs [we are quoting the words of a writer in the *Calcutta Review*] resting on a cane *moṛāh*. A long pipe, his most constant companion, projects from his mouth. A pair of loose *pyjamahs* and a *chārkhānah banyan* keep him within the pale of society and preserve him cool in the trying hot season of this climate. A rattan, his sceptre, is in his hand and the boys are seated on stools or little *moṛāhs* before his pedagogic majesty. They have already read three chapters of the Bible and have got over the proper names without much spelling; they have written their copies—small, round, text and large hands; they have repeated a column of Entick's Dictionary with only two mistakes; and are now employed in working Compound Division, and soon expect to arrive at the Rule of Three. Some of the lads' eyes are red with weeping and others expect to have a taste of the ferula. The partner of the pensioner's days is seated on a low Dinapore matronly chair, picking vegetables and preparing the ingredients for the coming dinner. It strikes 12 o'clock and the schoolmaster shakes himself. Presently, the boys bestir themselves, and for the day the school is broken up.'"[1]

[1] Carey's *Good Old Days of Hon. John Company*, Vol. I., pp. 396, 397.

Chapter I. — Other Educational Institutions.

There were, indeed, several schools of this sort formed for the instruction of youths of both sexes, but there were at the same time other institutions, the objects of which were serious and laudable and not mere money-making, through which their founders tried to give effect to their honest purposes in spite of the many obstacles in their way. Their real aim was dissemination of knowledge and qualifying the children for earning their livelihood by giving them a decent general education. Of course, success varied according to the means they could command for conducting the school.

(e) *Other Educational Institutions.*

We shall now proceed to give an account of the schools and colleges of the eighteenth century, besides those we have already noticed.

The Calcutta Madrasah was founded in 1781 by Warren Hastings, who paid for the building of the college premises out of his own pocket and at whose recommendation the Government assigned lands to the value of Rs.29,000/- per annum. The object of the founder was the encouragement of Arabic learning and the teaching of Muhammadan Law. The institution was not, however, successful and had to be remodelled in 1820.[1]

In 1788 Mr. Brown conducted a boarding-school for young Hindus. The school, however, had a brief existence. It may be remarked that Mr. Brown was made Provost of the newly established Fort William College in 1800.[2]

One Mr. Archer started a school for boys in 1780.[3] Others followed his example, as, for instance, Mr. Drummond (who was the first to introduce the system of annual public examinations and the use of globes in the schools), Messrs. Farrell, Halifax,

[1] Carey's *Good Old Days of Hon. John Company*, Vol. II., p. 160, and Vol. I., p. 411.

[2] Hyde's *Parochial Annals*, pp. 252, 262.

[3] *Calcutta Review* (1913), p. 340.

Chapter I.

Other Educational Institutions.

Lindstedt, Draper, Martin Bowles, Sherbourne, the Rev. Dr. Yates, etc. Mr. George Furly established an academy on the Burying Ground Road (now called Park Street) about 1793 and advertised the following three rates for board, lodging, and education, viz.: Rs.30/-, Rs.40/-, and Rs.64/-.[1]

The Rev. Mr. Holmes advertised in December, 1795, his academy at 74, Cossytullah Street, intended for the instruction of youths in the different branches of useful education. In the same year, Mr. W. Gaynard, Accountant, started an academy "at his house, No. 11, Meredith's Buildings, for a few gentlemen of the age of fourteen or upwards (who may be intended for the mercantile line of life) to instruct them in a perfect knowledge of Decimal calculations, and also to complete their education in the Italian

[1] *Calcutta Review* (1913), pp. 340, 341; and Carey's *Good Old Days of Hon. John Company*, Vol. I., p. 397.

method of Book-keeping, by a process using the weights, measures and coins of the different markets of India."[1]

In 1788 Mr. Mackinnon advertised a school to receive 140 pupils, and J. T. Hope opened another. In 1795 the Calcutta Academy was removed from Old Court House Street to the house in Chitpore Road known as Henry Tolfrey's.[2] Major-General Kirkpatrick founded the Military Orphan Society in March, 1783, for the maintenance and education of the destitute children of officers and soldiers. The society had two educational institutions, viz. the upper and the lower Orphan schools, the former for the children of officers and the latter for those of soldiers. There were two departments in each school[3] for boys and girls respectively,

1 Carey's *Good Old Days of Hon. John Company*, Vol. I., p. 398.

2 *Calcutta Review* (1913), p. 340.

3 Carey's *Good Old Days of Hon. John Company*, Vol. I., p. 401.

Military Orphan School (or Kirkpatrick's School). (From the *History, etc.*, *of Charitable Institutions*, by C. Lushington, 1824.)

Chapter I.

Female Education.

and the education imparted was designed to qualify the children for the situations they were likely to fill in India. The schools were first located at Howrah, but about 1790 they were removed to Kidderpore. They were in a very flourishing condition in 1795.[1]

(f) *Female Education.*

There are many rival claimants to the honour of having started the first girls' school in Calcutta. In his *Historical and Topographical Sketch of Calcutta*, Rainey says that the first girls' school was established in 1760 by one Mrs. Hedges. Here French and dancing were taught. The lady retired in 1780 with a snug fortune. Captain Williamson mentions in his *East India Vade Mecum* that one "Mrs. Hodges" founded the first ladies' seminary in 1780. In spite of the difference as to the date of establishment

[1] Carey's *Good Old Days of Hon. John Company*, Vol. I., p. 401.

of the institution, it seems that the two accounts contemplate the same school and that Mrs. Hodges was no other than Mrs. Hedges.[1] Moreover, Mr. Carey says in his *Good Old Days of Hon. John Company* that the earliest school for young ladies was that of Mrs. Pitts. The writer of the *Hartley House* (1789) mentions a girls' school conducted by Mrs. Savage, the only one in Calcutta, much in esteem with the Europeans.[2] Amid this medley of claims, it is difficult to decide who should be credited with the honour. Leaving it to be decided by others, let us turn to other girls' schools that were established. One was started by Mrs. Durrell. This seminary was situated in Clive Street and enjoyed the most extensive support.[3] Mrs. Copeland opened a young ladies'

1 *Calcutta Review* (1913), p. 343. Mr. Carey mentions a girls' school established by Mrs. Lawson. This was, however, founded about 1812—see *Calcutta Review*, July, 1913, p. 343.

2 *Ibid.*, p. 343.

3 *Ibid.*, p. 398.

school in 1792. It was located in the house nearly opposite to Mr. Nicholas Charles' Europe Shop. Here girls were taught reading, writing and needle-work. John Stansberrow opened a mixed school for boys and girls in a garden-house at Mirzapore in 1785. The children were taught reading, writing and arithmetic, the girls being in addition trained in lace-making and needle-work. The terms were as follows :—

For a boy . . .	Rs.25/-	per month.
For a girl . . .	„ 30/-	„
For a day-scholar	„ 16/-	„

At first, only 12 boys and 12 girls were taken into the school, in order that they might obtain the best attention of the masters.[1] Mrs. Pyne also kept a boarding-school for girls which, it appears from an advertisement in the *Calcutta Gazette*,

[1] Carey's *Good Old Days of Hon. John Company*, pp. 398, 399 ; and *Calcutta Review* (1913), p. 340.

was removed to a house in Dacre's Lane in 1794.[1]

(g) *Asiatic Society of Bengal.*

For diffusion of historical and scientific knowledge, the Asiatic Society of Bengal was established on the 15th January, 1784, by the celebrated linguist, naturalist and jurist, Sir William Jones. The papers that were read in its weekly evening meetings were published in its periodical called the *Asiatic Researches.* The founder himself was elected its first President, as Warren Hastings, the Governor-General, declined the offer of the chair. It is superfluous to add that the Society has done a good deal of useful work by extending the bounds of knowledge in almost all its departments.[2]

[1] *Calcutta Review* (1913), p. 343.

[2] Carey's *Good Old Days of Hon. John Company*, Vol. I., p. 417.

CHAPTER II.

EDUCATIONAL ACTIVITIES OUTSIDE CALCUTTA.

About this time, Calcutta and the neighbouring districts were not the only places where schools were established. Mrs. Middleton took a house in 1799 "in an airy, healthy and agreeable situation at Dinapore" for the tuition of both boys and girls, the fees being two gold *mohars* per month for boarders and Rs.8/- for day-scholars.[1]

A missionary school was established at Dinajpore by Mr. Carey in 1794. The number of scholars amounted to 40 in the third year after it was opened. The Baptist missionaries of Serampore were so very zealous in educational matters

[1] Carey's *Good Old Days of Hon. John Company*, Vol. I., p. 399.

that by 1817 no less than 115 schools were founded, the majority of which were within thirty miles of Calcutta, containing above ten thousand alumni.[1]

In 1794 a college was endowed at Benares on the recommendation of Mr. Duncan, afterwards Governor of Bombay, for the cultivation of Hindu literature.[2]

We have very few records about the educational institutions founded by Europeans in Northern India. Bernier, who visited India in the latter part of the seventeenth century, during the reign of Shāh Jahān, saw in Agra a college which had been established by the Jesuits for teaching the children of about thirty Christian families in the Christian doctrine. They had been invited to settle there by the Great Akbar, who allotted them an annual income for their maintenance.[3]

1 Carey's *Good Old Days of Hon. John Company*, Vol. I., p. 408.

2 *Ibid.*, p. 410.

3 Constable's *Bernier*, p. 286.

Conclusion.

CONCLUSION.

We are now in a position to estimate the amount of educational work done by the Europeans in this country up to the end of the eighteenth century. It was the chaplains and missionaries who were the most zealous in this matter; it was they who first recognized it as a duty to impart education to the people under their care in the European settlements and persuaded the authorities both here and at home to fulfil this duty not only by founding educational institutions on their own initiative, but also by helping the missionaries and private individuals by giving them aids, financial or otherwise. The names of those gentlemen who by their zeal and labour gave their whole-hearted support to this educational movement should never be forgotten. In judging of their work, we should look not merely to their accomplished deeds, which may be faulty, but to their motives as well.

It is true that the majority of the institutions founded by them imparted an education the standard of which was not very high; yet they served a very useful purpose. Higher education, however, was not altogether ignored, as provisions for such education were made in the colleges noticed before. When we take into account the difficulties that beset the undertakings of these people, we cannot help admiring their earnestness and making allowance if their "acts could not prove all their thoughts had been." The undaunted ardour and enthusiasm of men like Ziegenbalg, Grundler, Schultz, Fabricius, Schwartz, Bell, Kerr and Stevenson in Southern India, and Briercliffe, Kiernander and others in Northern India can surely stand comparison with those of the European educationists that have graced

Conclusion.

the nineteenth century. These personages would not now have been mere shadows of a forgotten past, if they could have worked in more favourable surroundings and have left behind them more accomplished works.

INDEX I.—SUBJECTS.

INDEX II.—PROPER NAMES AND LITERARY REFERENCES.

INDEX III.—CHRONOLOGICAL.